Tricks, Stunts & GOOD CLEAN FUN

Bob Phillips

HARVEST HOUSE PUBLISHERS
Eugene, Oregon 97402

Unless otherwise indicated, all Scripture references are taken from the King James Version of the Bible. Scripture reference marked NKJV is taken from the New King James Version, Copyright © 1979, 1980, 1982 by Thomas Nelson, Inc., Publishers. Used by permission.

Illustrated by Norm Daniels.

Contents

Introduction

Finally, it has happened. Bob Phillips has written so many joke books that it has warped his brain. In his twisted state of mind he has produced the ultimate in humorous entertainment . . . *Tricks, Stunts, and Good Clean Fun*. Foolishness has now become an art form.

This book is totally designed for anyone who never wants to grow up. It's guaranteed to drive friends, relatives, and innocent bystanders crazy.

Who dares to pick up this book?

- Dads and moms who want to entertain their children.

- Aunts and uncles who want to trick their nieces and nephews.

- Grandparents who want to baffle their grandchildren.

- Kids who want to drive their parents stark raving mad.

- Teachers who want to confuse their students.

- Youth leaders who want to pull gags on their youth group.

- Anyone who wants to bamboozle neighbors and play practical jokes on their friends.

At last, we have the final word in verbal hocus-pocus. You will gasp in wonder at the wild word puzzles. You will roll on the ground in laughter with the fun practical jokes. Your eyes will crisscross at the optical illusions.

Great reviews are already coming in.

"You've got to be kidding."
"I can't believe my eyes!"
"Sneaky, sneaky."
"I can't take any more!"

Don't stop now! Get ready to start learning the many wild and harmless ways to fool your family and flimflam your friends. Amaze them by your ability to make sense out of nonsense. Become an expert in wacky humor.

This book is so fantastic that it has helped me write these clever lines. It even helped me move into a new home on the "farm." In fact, they let me out for a few minutes so I could write these words.

Come and visit me and my friends some time. You will love George Washington—he lives next door. And Napoleon just moved in across the hall.

—Bob Phillips
Inmate, Fresno Funny Farm

Tricks, Stunts, and Good Clean Fun

brain-benders

1. The animals of nature are quite interesting. Which one of the following animals can see most clearly in total darkness? A leopard, a bat, or an owl?

2. Hollywood, California is known for a lot of unusual things. Recently, a woman from Hollywood married ten different men, yet she did not break any laws. None of the men died; she did not divorce any of them. How did this unusual thing happen?

3. In California there is a small town where 7% of all the people living in the town have unlisted phone numbers. The town has 3,500 people living in it. If you selected 100 names at random from the town's phone directory, on average, how many of these people selected would have unlisted phone numbers?

4. Before Australia was discovered, what was the largest island?

5. Gary was in charge of a chemistry laboratory. One day Danny, a chemist in the lab, came to him with a large flask in his hand. He said, "I have just discovered a liquid so powerful that it will instantly dissolve anything it touches! I've made enough of it to fill a flask half full." Gary responded, "Danny, you're fired. I don't keep employees working for me that lie." How did Gary know Danny was lying?

6. Abraham Lincoln was known for his great sense of humor. He gave his wife a bottomless container to put flesh and blood in. What did President Lincoln give to Mary Todd Lincoln?

7. The maker of the product does not want it. The buyer of the product doesn't use it. The user of the product doesn't see it. It's used every day around the world. What is it?

8. A great golfer was playing in a match when all of a sudden it began to rain. It was a cloudburst. Soon the golf course was soaked. His caddy was soaked. Everybody that was watching was soaked. The golfer did not have an umbrella and he wasn't wearing a hat. His clothes were sopping wet, yet not a hair on his head got wet. How was that possible?

9. How many different species of mammals, birds, and reptiles did Moses take onto the ark with him?

10. At Sloppy Sam's Restaurant, Willard was shocked to find a fly in his coffee. He sent the waiter back for a fresh cup. The waiter returned and gave Willard the cup. After his first sip, Willard pounded on the table and shouted: "This is the same cup of coffee I had before!" How could Willard tell it was the same cup of coffee?

11. Mr. Know-It-All was asked the following questions: How many grooves are there on each side of a standard 33⅓ record album that has seven songs on each side?

12. A 10-volume encyclopedia stands on the shelf as shown below. Each volume is two inches thick. Suppose a bookworm starts at the front cover of volume 1 and eats his way in a straight horizontal line through to the back cover of volume 10. How far does the worm travel?

Vol 1	Vol 2	Vol 3	Vol 4	Vol 5	Vol 6	Vol 7	Vol 8	Vol 9	Vol 10

13. A great hunter was walking in the jungle without his rifle. All of a sudden he heard a noise behind him. He turned and saw a large tiger coming after him. He knew that his only way of escape was to get into some water because tigers don't like to chase their prey in water. The hunter made a quick dash directly toward the tiger. He ran toward him for a short while, then fled to some water for safety. Why did the hunter run toward the tiger?

14. What is the beginning of eternity . . . the end of time
. . . the beginning of every end . . . and the end of
every place?

15. Mr. Know-It-All was asked: In the following series
of numbers, which ones can be divided by two?
1 2 3 4 5 6 7 8 9 10
What was Mr. Know-It All's answer?

16. Mr. West went for a hike in a very dense and dark
forest. Towards evening he made camp, ate dinner,
and got ready for bed. During the middle of the
night he got up to put some more wood on the fire.
As he got out of his sleeping bag he felt something
move in the pocket of his shorts. It had a head and
tail, but no legs. He stopped for a second as it
moved. He then put some wood on the fire, got
back into his sleeping bag and went to sleep. Why
did Mr. West show so little concern?

17. See if you can match these familiar sayings.

1. Fit as _____	A. A razor
2. Flat as _____	B. A bell
3. Blind as _____	C. A peacock
4. Light as _____	D. A rock
5. Happy as _____	E. A church mouse
6. Cold as _____	F. An eel
7. Cool as _____	G. A pin
8. Fat as _____	H. Silk
9. Poor as _____	I. A whip
10. Rich as _____	J. A pancake
11. Patient as _____	K. Punch
12. Stubborn as _____	L. A hog in new mud
13. Proud as _____	M. A dollar

14. Dead as _____   N. Thieves
15. Hard as _____   O. A king
16. Soft as _____   P. A bat
17. Clear as _____   Q. Job
18. Slippery as _____   R. A cucumber
19. Sharp as _____   S. A feather
20. Smart as _____   T. A mule
21. Clean as _____   U. A fiddle
22. Pleased as _____   V. Ice
23. Busy as _____   W. A doornail
24. Neat as _____   X. A whistle
25. Sound as_____   Y. A bee
26. Thick as _____   Z. A hog

bible riddles #1

1. What was the name of Isaiah's horse?

2. Who was the first man in the Bible to know the meaning of rib roast?

3. Where does it talk about Honda cars in the Bible?

4. Who is the smallest man in the Bible?

5. Where in the Bible does it say that we should not play marbles?

6. How were Adam and Eve prevented from gambling?

7. Where in the Bible does it say we shouldn't fly in airplanes?

8. What did Noah say while he was loading all the animals on the Ark?

9. When did Jacob sleep with five people in one bed?

party fun

Nine Magazines

You will need nine magazines and a pointer of some kind for this trick. (A yardstick or a broom handle will do as a pointer.) Place the nine magazines on the floor in three rows with three magazines in each row.

Explain to the group that you have great mental powers. You have the ability to know which of the nine magazines on the floor the group has chosen. To prove your great ability, choose someone from the group and give them the pointer.

Tell the group to choose any one of the magazines on the floor while you are out of the room. When the pointer calls you back in, have him point at any magazine and ask, "Is this the one?" The pointer person should ask the same question every time he points to a magazine. You, in turn will answer yes or no.

This trick is made simple because the person you choose to be the pointer is your accomplice. He also knows the trick.

The first magazine your accomplice points at will give you the answer. As you look at any of the magazines on the floor draw an imaginary grid over that magazine.

Make the imaginary grid the same as the nine magazines on the floor . . . three rows with three in every row (see illustration below).

It is now up to your pointer to do the job of telling you which magazine was chosen by the group. He will choose one magazine on the floor and point to it. If he points to the center of the magazine, you know the group chose #5, the center of the magazines on the floor. If he points to the upper-right corner of the magazine, you know the group chose #3, the upper-right magazine on the floor. If he points to the bottom center of the magazine, you know that the group chose #8, the bottom center of the magazines on the floor. The pointer should be pointing in a casual manner so the group won't see what the pointer is doing for you.

You will be able to do this trick a number of times without the group catching on. If someone in the group knows how the trick is done, ask him to not let anyone know. We suggest you stop after about six times. Be sure not to give away your secret.

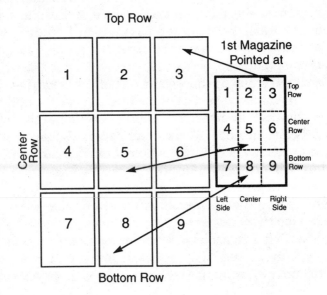

the guessing game

This is a good trick for a party. You will need an accomplice. Your accomplice will tell the group that you have great mental powers and can read minds.

Your accomplice will ask you to leave the room while the group agrees on an object for you to identify. When you come back into the room, your accomplice will point to different objects in the room and ask, "Is that it?" He will point to a number of different objects to which you will respond, "No." When he points to the object that the group has chosen, you will say, "Yes." Then you can leave the room and perform the trick again. Be sure not to drag the trick on too long. Do not give away the secret.

Your secret is that you and your accomplice have agreed to use the letter "c" as your cue. When your accomplice points to an object that starts with "c," the next object pointed at will be the object chosen by the group. For instance, your friend will point to a couch and you will say, "That's not it." Then he will point to the correct object and you will say, "That's it!" You don't have to use the letter "c" as your cue, you can use a color like blue, and so on.

After you do the trick four times, change it a little.

Upon your return to the room, have your accomplice say, "Now, I am going to point to five different objects.

I don't want you to say anything until I have pointed them out. When I am finished, you can try to identify what the group has selected." You still use the same "c" cue or "blue" cue as before. The reason for the change is to throw the group off as they are trying to figure out how the trick works.

spots before your eyes

If you look at the two drawings below you will begin to see spots before your eyes. As you look at the black lines you will see little light gray spots come and go; as you look at the white lines you will see little dark gray spots come and go.

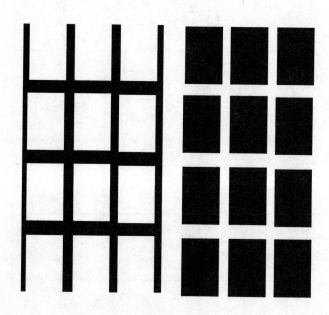

21

Can you identify these word puzzles?

<table>
<tr><td>

Mr. E

</td><td>

E G E
   G
G S
     S
E G E

</td><td>

!
S
D
N
A
H

</td></tr>
<tr><td>

DIG CLUE
     CLUE
     CLUE
     CLUE

</td><td>

AAGGEENNTT

</td><td>

ARREST
——————
U R

</td></tr>
<tr><td>

T
H
E
CROOK

</td><td>

THE WAKE UP NIGHT

</td><td>

CRIPARTNERSME

</td></tr>
</table>

crazy pictures quiz #1

See if you can identify the pictures below . . .

The Swimming Egg

You will need two glasses of water and an egg. Hand one of the glasses of water to your friend. Ask your friend to take the egg and see if he can teach it to swim. Have him put his egg into his glass of water and see if it will swim on top of the water or sink to the bottom.

When he puts the egg into the glass of water, it will sink to the bottom. Have him try a couple of times.

Then say to your friend, "You just don't know how to teach swimming lessons. You have to whisper into the egg's "ear" and tell him how to do it." You then take the same egg and whisper into the egg's ear (say anything you want). If you want to have some fun, whisper loud enough for your friend to hear. You could say something like, "I'm sorry that mean old person almost let you drown. I won't let that happen to you. Now, you do the backstroke I told you about and you will stay afloat."

Gently put the egg into your glass of water. As it floats say, "See, isn't that better. I knew you could do it. You're a good egg." Your friend's mouth will drop open. He will probably ask, "How did you do that?"

Just smile and say, "You have to be kind and loving and know how to deal with sensitive eggs." Then you take the egg out of the water and hand it to your friend. Then pour out the two glasses of water.

The secret to the swimming egg lies in the fact that you put salt into the glass that you were holding *before* you showed the trick to your friend. When you prepare the glass of salt water, be sure that the salt has been stirred until it has dissolved. You will have to test the egg in your salt water several times to see if you have enough salt to make it float.

If the salt has dissolved ahead of time, both glasses of water will be the same. Be sure that you hold on to the one that has the salt water in it. Pour out the water of both glasses after the trick—you don't want your friend to grab your glass and put his egg into it. Don't tell him your secret. It will be fun to be the one in the know and leave him hanging in the air!

Karate Chop

You will need a soda pop bottle or a bottle with an opening about the size of a quarter for this trick. You will also need a strip of paper about 2 inches wide by 11 inches long and four quarters. Place one end of the piece of paper on the top to the bottle. Take the four quarters and stack them on top of the piece of paper, right over the bottle opening.

Ask your friends if they can pull the paper out from under the quarters

25

without the quarters falling off the top of the bottle. Let them try a few times before you show them the trick.

The secret to remove the paper is in a "karate chop." Hold the paper level with one hand. Give a quick karate chop, striking the paper in the middle. The paper will come out and the coins will remain on top of the bottle. Practice this trick a couple of times before showing your friends. Have fun!

You're All Wet

Get a paper napkin, a glass, and a bowl of water that is deeper than the glass for this trick. Place the bowl of water and napkin in front of you. Set the glass nearby—not too close to the bowl of water or the paper napkin. You want your friends to think that you are just using the napkin and bowl of water.

Tell your friends, "I can put this paper napkin completely under water in this bowl and it won't get wet."

Your friends will probably say, "No way!" Simply smile and say, "Yes, I can."

Then crumple the paper napkin up in a ball and pretend you are going to put it into the bowl of water. Hesitate for a moment and then grab the nearby glass. Stuff the napkin in the glass, pushing it to the bottom. Turn the glass over so that the rim of the glass enters the water. Shove the glass straight down under the water. The air pocket in the glass will keep the paper napkin completely dry. You might want to practice this a few times before amazing your friends.

The Balancing Half-Dollar

You will need a glass, a 50-cent piece (a quarter will work but makes the trick a little harder to perform) and two forks for this trick. Place the 50-cent piece between the first and second tines of both forks (see page 27).

Next, place the 50-cent piece on the edge of the glass. Carefully move the forks back and forth until you get a balance—hang the two forks on half of the 50-cent piece while the other edge balances on the edge of the glass. It can be done! Behold! the amazing balancing half-dollar.

Blackbird Buddies

Take a dollar bill and fold it in thirds with the ends hanging out (like the drawing below). Then place the first paper clip on the bill (holding the back and second fold together). Tell your friend that this is a blackbird sitting on a fence. Then place the second paper clip on the bill and tell your friend that this is a second blackbird sitting on a fence. They were lonely so they decided to fly together.

As soon as you say this, quickly pull both ends of the dollar bill at the same time. The paper clips will join together and come flying off the dollar bill!

Pinocchio

Place a coin in one of your friend's hands. Ask him to put his hands behind his back. Tell him to switch the coin into either his right hand or left hand, but not tell you which.

Then have him bring his hands forward with closed fists and hold his arms out at shoulder level. Ask him to concentrate on the hand that holds the coin—still not telling you where it is. After a moment tell him which hand holds the coin.

This trick will work most of the time if you are very careful. Keep your eyes on your friend's nose. His nose will . . . ever so slightly . . . point toward the hand holding the coin. If you cannot see the slight movement of his nose, have him do it again.

If you have him do it again say, "I don't think you are concentrating. Try it again." You will be surprised how many times you can guess correctly and so will your friend.

Showing Appreciation

Take someone's business card (your parents may have one) and bend one corner up (about a quarter of an inch) and the opposite corner down about a quarter of an inch. Place the business card on the edge of a table.

Tell your friend that you can turn the business card over just by showing appreciation. Inform him that you will not touch the card. He will want to see a demonstration.

Clapping is a form of showing appreciation. Simply clap your hands together. The wind from the clapping will turn the business card over. Practice this trick a couple of times before you try it on your friends.

How About a Drink

You will need two glasses and a saucer for this trick. Fill one of the glasses half-full with water, soda pop, or some other drink. Put the saucer on top of the half-filled glass. Then set the empty glass on top of the saucer

Say to your friend, "I'll bet you can't drink the water in the bottom glass! Here are the rules:

1. Don't touch either the top glass or the saucer with your hands, lips, teeth, or any part of your body.
2. You can touch anything else in the room except the empty glass and the saucer.
3. You cannot ask anyone else to help you remove the empty glass or the saucer.
4. You must hold on to the half-full glass at all times until you get a drink from it."

Hand the two glasses and saucer to your friend, making sure he is holding only the half-full glass in his hand. Tell him to begin. Let him struggle with it for a while then tell him, "When you are ready to give up, I'll show you how to do it."

The trick is very simple. Just place the glass between two boxes, a stack of books, or any two objects of the same size and taller than the bottom glass. Make sure the two objects are fairly close together. Once the saucer is on the two objects, remove the bottom glass and take a drink.

Tricks, Stunts, and Good Clean Fun

reverse arrows

As you study the two drawings below, determine which horizontal line is longer than the other.

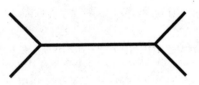

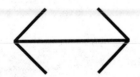

bible riddles #2

1. What was the first theatrical event in the Bible?

2. Where in the Bible does it say that fathers should let their sons use the car?

3. Why are there so few men with whiskers in heaven?

4. Who was the best financier in the Bible?

5. What simple affliction brought about the death of Samson?

6. What did Adam and Eve do when they were expelled from the Garden of Eden?

7. What are two of the smallest insects mentioned in the Bible?

8. In what place did the cock crow when everyone in the world could hear him?

9. What were the Phoenicians famous for?

10. Where is deviled ham mentioned in the Bible?

Tricks, Stunts, and Good Clean Fun

practical jokes

The Genius Quiz

Make a copy of the following little quiz. Then hand your friend the quiz, along with a piece of paper and a pen or pencil. See if he can complete the following test in record time.

The Genius Quiz

1. Read everything that follows before you begin.
2. Print your name in the upper right-hand corner of the paper.
3. Draw a box around your last name.
4. Put an "X" before and after your name.
5. In the middle of the paper write, "I see a cat in a tree."
6. Put a circle around any letter "a" in the sentence you just wrote in the middle of the paper.
7. Write "I am smart" under the sentence "I see a cat in a tree."
8. At the bottom of the page, write the alphabet.
9. Up the left side of the paper write the numbers "1, 2, 3, 4, 5, 6, 7, 8, 9, 10" starting from the bottom and going up.

10. Circle any odd numbers you just wrote down.
11. Draw a square around the number 6.
12. Say out loud, "I'm almost finished and I have followed all the directions carefully."
13. Now that you have finished reading carefully, do only sentences 1, 2, and 13.

Mountaintop

Ask your friends to point a finger to the side of their head. Ask them to count to ten. Then have them tell you who the first president of the United States was. Next, ask them to give you the abbreviation for the state of Washington. Ask them to give you the abbreviation for the city of New York. Finally, ask them to give you the abbreviation for mountain.

"MT."

Then say, "You're right—it's empty up there!" as you point to their head.

It's a Bird

This is an old trick but it is lots of fun. You can do this by yourself, but it works better if you have a friend with you. You will be able to enjoy the laugh together.

When you find yourself at school, on a busy corner, in a shopping mall—almost anywhere—stand still and look up. Every now and then point and talk to each other. Pretend that you are looking at something up in the air or that something is happening on a tall wall or building.

Soon everyone around you will begin to look up also. They will be trying to see what you are looking at. After you get enough people looking up, walk away and have a good laugh.

Smatter

Here's an easy way to get a laugh. Turn to your friend and ask, "Have you ever bought a smatter at the mall?"

"What's a smatter?"

"Nothing. What's a smatter with you?"

Short Sheet

This is a good prank to pull at camp (or on your brother or sister at home). It's called short sheeting the bed.

Start by unmaking the bed. Put down the bottom sheet (make sure it's a flat sheet) but not a top sheet. Fold the bottom of the sheet up toward the top so that it will look like two sheets. Then put the blankets back on the bed and make it look like normal.

When your victim goes to bed, he will turn back the covers and try to slip into bed. But he won't be able to stretch out his legs because of the fold in the sheet! He will struggle and be confused until the light finally dawns and he realizes he's the victim of a practical joke.

Snoo

Another laugh and groan will follow this conversation. Turn to your friend and warn, "Watch out! Don't step on the Snoo."

"What's a Snoo?"

"Not much. What's snoo with you?"

Be Careful

Find a small box that has a lid on it. Make a little sign to put on the outside of the box that reads:

DANGER
THIS BOX CONTAINS A BIG BLACK BEE
WITH TWO GREEN EYES
OPEN AT YOUR OWN RISK

Inside the box put a little card with the letter "B" written very large. On each side of the letter "B" write a lower case letter "i" using green ink.

Set the box in a conspicuous place and watch the fun.

Henweigh

Here's another verbal volley! Turn to your friend and ask, "Would you like to see my Henweigh?

"What's a Henweigh?"

"Oh, about three or four pounds."

Wacky Word

Turn to your friend and say, "I know that you are a good speller, but I found an eight-letter word that I don't think you can spell." Be sure to say the following phrase exactly as it is written—this will help to confuse your friend even more.

"The middle 3 letters of this word are *k–s–t*, in the beginning, and at the end."

Your friend will probably say, "Say that again. I don't think there is any word like that."

"The middle 3 letters of this word are *k–s–t*, in the beginning, and at the end." Let them struggle with it for a little while.

Then say to your friend, "Let me give you a clue. In the 1700s a feather was often involved with this word." Now they will really be confused.

"I'll give you another clue. In the early 1900's a pen was usually used." Let them struggle for a while and then say, "Do you give up?" When they do, repeat the original phrase. Tell them to listen very carefully. As you repeat the phrase, pause after each comma.

"The middle 3 letters of this word are *k–s–t*, (pause) *in* the beginning, (pause) *and* at the end."

He will probably still look at you funny. Simply say, "The word is inkstand. An inkstand was used with both feathers and pens. *In* is the beginning, *k–s–t* is the middle, *and* is at the end. *Inkstand*."

On Fire

This prank is as old as the hills. If your friend's shirt is tucked in, turn to him and say, "Your shirttail's on fire!"

Quickly pull your friend's shirt out of his pants and say, "Now it's out."

The Triple "T" Test

Ask your friend to help you with the Triple "T" Test. Begin by saying,

"What do the letters T–O spell?"

"To."

"How many fingers am I holding up?" (Hold up two.)

"Two."

"What is the name of the famous author who's first name is Mark and he wrote *Huckleberry Finn*?"

"Twain."

"Very good. Now let me hear you say all three answers in a row."

"To, Two, Twain."

"Please say it again."

"To, Two, Twain."

"One more time, only faster."

"To, Two, Twain."

"That's great. You're learning to play 'railroad'."

Melvin and Willard

Here is a little practical joke rhyme that is as old as the hills. It has been used many, many times. Say to your friend:

> Melvin, Willard, and Pinch-Me
> Went out on a lake in a boat.
> Melvin fell out of the boat.
> Willard dove in after him to save him.
> Who was left in the boat?

As soon as your friend says, "Pinch-Me," go ahead and pinch him.

crazy pie

Study the pie below. See if you can just look at the black pieces and not the white pieces.

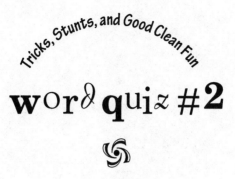

Tricks, Stunts, and Good Clean Fun

word quiz #2

See if you can identify these word puzzles.

KNEE LIGHTS	**P R O S P E R I T Y**	**DR.** **DR.**
WAY YIELD	**APPOD**	**PRICE**
G H O N R I S	*EVERYTHING PIZZA*	**ZZZZZZ** **XX**

39

crazy pictures
quiz #2

Can you identify the pictures below?

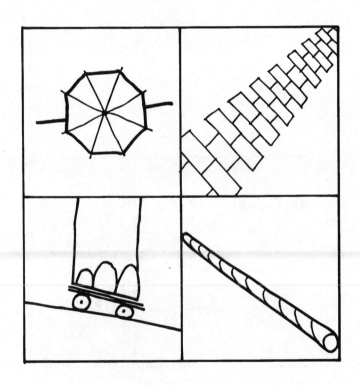

flimflam

The Car Athlete

Turn to your friend and say, "I'll bet I can jump as high as this car from a standing position." (Turn and point to a car parked nearby.)

Your friend will probably say, "I'll bet you can't."

You respond by saying, "I'll bet I can." Then look at your friend and say, "Cars can't jump."

Easy Money

The next time you are at a restaurant with your friend, you can make some easy money.

Have your friend put a quarter on a clean plate.

Ask your friend, "If I can get the quarter off the plate without touching the table, the plate, or the quarter, may I have it?" Tell your friend that you will not use any object of any kind to help you remove the quarter.

He will probably study the matter for a few minutes and then ask you some questions. Eventually he will probably agree—a quarter is not much to lose.

Take a deep breath and *blow* the quarter off the plate. Be sure the plate you select doesn't have steep edges.

Sometimes when you blow, the quarter will move to the edge of the plate and not quite go over the edge. It will bounce a little. If that happens, take another quick, deep breath and blow hard while the coin is still slightly bouncing. This second gust of wind should do the trick. Practice a few times before you try it with your friend.

A Nickel for Your Trouble

Place three coins in a straight line on a table in front of you. Use a penny, a nickel, and another penny. Place the nickel between the pennies.

Tell your friend that without touching the nickel you can move it to the right of both of the pennies. Explain that you will not touch the nickel, blow on the nickel, or move the nickel with any object.

Your friend will probably say, "I'll bet you can't do it." Just smile and say, "I bet I can."

Say some made-up "magic" words, then pick up the penny on the right and move it to the other side, next to the penny on the left. This moves the nickel to the right of both pennies—just like you said.

A Breathless Trick

This is a good trick to do when you are at the beach or near a swimming pool. Turn to your friend and say, "I'll bet you that I can stay under water for five minutes."

They may respond by saying something like, "You can't hold your breath that long."

Ignore their comment and repeat, "I can stay under water for five minutes."

"I'll bet you can't. Let's see you do it."

Then pick up a glass or cup of water and hold it over your head for five minutes.

The Balancing Glass

For this flimflam fun you will need three glasses and a sheet of notebook paper. You can even use a three-by-five card if you want.

Show the three glasses and the piece of paper to your friends. Tell them that you can balance the piece of paper on the edges between two glasses and then place the third glass on the paper without the third glass falling to the ground.

Your friends will jump at this challenge and say, "I bet you can't do it."

Take the piece of paper and fold it in an accordion fold (about ½" wide). Crease the folds so they are tight. Next, place the accordion folded paper between the two glasses. Then carefully place the third glass on top of the accordion folded paper. The paper should be strong enough to hold up the glass even if it's full of water. Be sure to practice this trick a couple of times before you pull it on your friends.

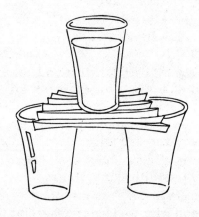

Overweight

In the presence of your friend, take two pieces of paper (notebook paper is a good size) and hand them to your friend. Tell him to stand and hold one piece of paper in each hand. Ask him to let go of both pieces of paper at the same time and watch them drop to the ground.

Tell him that if you make one of the pieces of paper overweight that it will fall to the ground faster than the other piece. Then take one of the pieces of paper and write "overweight" on it.

Turn to your friend and say, "Now that I have written the word overweight on one piece, do you think it will fall to the ground faster than the one with nothing written on it?" He will probably say no. You respond by saying, "I'll bet it will."

Take the piece of paper with the word "overweight" on it and crumple it up into a tight ball. Then hold both pieces of paper at the same height and let them go at the same time. The crumpled piece of paper will fall directly to the ground while the other piece will slowly float to the ground.

The Special Touch

Turn to a friend and say, "I'll bet I can touch a book outside and inside without opening it."

Your friend will probably say, "No way!"

Respond by saying, "I'll bet I can."

Then step outside the room or house, touch the book, then step back inside the room or house and touch it again.

Multiplying Money

This is a good trick to do at a restaurant with a number of friends. Tell your friends to each take out a quarter and look at the date. Then have them place their quarters on the table so that the date cannot be seen by you.

Tell your friends that you are willing to pay a dime for every quarter whose date you can't name . . . without looking at the quarters. Be sure to have a number of dimes in your pocket. Pull the dimes out and place them on the table in front of you. Ask them to leave the quarter on the table until you have tried to guess all the coins. Of course you will not be able to guess any of the quarters correctly.

One by one go around the table and guess the date of the quarter. Each time after you guess, have your friend turn his quarter over. You will have guessed the wrong date. Your friend will feel good. When you are finished guessing all the coins, ask your friends to let you look at the dates. This gets the quarters in front of you. As you look at each coin say, "I didn't get this one."

Then look at your friends and say, "I'm going to keep my word. I told you that I would pay a dime for every quarter whose date I could not guess. Hand each of your friends a dime, and say, "I'm paying you dimes for quarters. Then quickly put the quarters in your pocket. If you are sitting in a booth be sure you are sitting on the outside so you can escape with your life.

Super Strength

Hand your friend a large telephone book. (This needs to be an old telephone book that is no longer in use.) Ask him to tear the book in half. Let him try it for a little while before giving up.

Then say, "I'll bet I can tear the telephone book in half." They will respond, "I'll bet you can't." You answer, "I'll bet I can."

You then take the telephone book, open it in the middle and tear it in half—down the binding (not through the pages).

Subtraction Magic

Take a pen and piece of paper and place them in front of your friend. Say, "I'll bet that I can subtract four from four and be left with eight."

Your friend won't believe you. Tell him you can do it.

Take the piece of paper and fold over all four corners (use small to medium folds). Tear off the triangle pieces on the folds. Move the four torn off pieces into a pile. Hand the piece of paper to your friend and point out that, "I have subtracted four corners from four corners of the piece of paper. Now look at the paper. It now has eight corners. Four from four leaves eight."

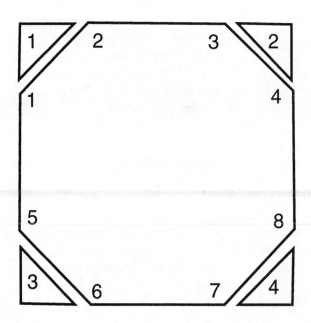

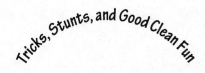

bible riddles #3

1. Who introduced the first walking stick?

2. When is medicine first mentioned in the Bible?

3. Where in the Bible does it suggest that men should wash dishes?

4. Where did Noah strike the first nail in the ark?

5. Why was Moses the most wicked man in the Bible?

6. What man in the Bible spoke when he was a very small baby?

7. At what time of day was Adam born?

8. What man in the Bible had no parents?

9. Where is tennis mentioned in the Bible?

10. Was there any money on Noah's ark?

crazy stunts

Name, Address, and Phone Number

Have your friend sit down at a table that has a piece of paper and a pen or pencil on it.

Ask your friend to print her name, address, and phone number on the piece of paper in front of them. After she follows those instructions, have her take her right foot and make clockwise circles with it. The foot circles should be about the size of a dinner plate.

Tell your friend to keep making small circles with her foot and again write her name, address, and phone number on the paper. She must do both activities at the same time and not stop until the writing assignment is finished.

You will all get a big laugh. Your friend will not be able to do it nor will you be able to read anything she wrote.

Grabbing for Money

Hold your elbow at shoulder height. Turn your palm down toward your shoulder. Place a number of coins on top of each other on the inside top of your elbow. Now drop the coins off of your elbow and see if you can catch them with the same hand.

Once you have mastered this stunt, spread the coins from your elbow all the way up your arm. Then try to drop them off and catch all of them. Keep adding coins up your arm to see how many you can catch without dropping them. This would be a great contest between you and your friends to see who can catch the most coins.

Waiting in Line

We have all found ourselves waiting in line. However, with this stunt we want you to wait in line . . . standing on one foot . . . with your eyes closed . . . for one full minute.

See if you can do this stunt without putting your foot down. Have a friend time you for one minute since your eyes will be closed.

Magic Eye Glue

Tell your friend that you have some magic eye glue. Explain that when you sprinkle it on his eyes he will not be able to open them. Of course he won't believe you.

Have your friend look straight forward. Next, have him lift his eyes so he is looking up at the ceiling—but without moving his head.

Sprinkle some imaginary "eye glue" over his eyes and tell him to close his eyes but keep looking up. Ask if he is looking up while his eyes are closed. When he says yes tell him to keep looking up but open his eyelids. It is impossible to look up and open the eyelids at the same time. Tell your friend it was the Magic Eye Glue that you used.

The Big Bass Drum

Here is a challenge that none of your friends will be able to do. Ask your friends to imagine that they have a big bass drum in front of them. Have them stick their arms out in front of them.

Tell them to take their right hand and move it around the edge of the imaginary drum. Their right hand will begin to go around in a circle. Tell them to keep their right hand going around while they move their left hand around the edge of the imaginary drum in the opposite direction.

Next, have your friends keep moving their hands in circles while drawing a circle with the toe of their right foot.

This is an impossible trick to perform.

the magic staircase

Start at one of the corners of the staircase and determine which is the bottom step. Once you find the bottom step, start climbing the steps until you get to the top step.

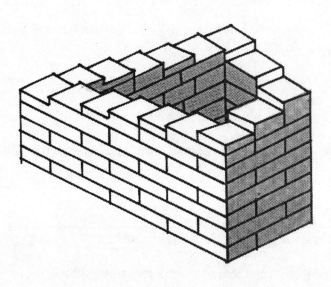

51

bib/e rid∂les #4

1. Paul, the apostle, was a great preacher and teacher and earned his living as a tentmaker. What other occupation did Paul have?

2. Why was Adam's first day the longest?

3. Why was a woman in the Bible turned into a pillar of salt?

4. What story in the Bible talks about a very lazy man?

5. Why didn't the last dove return to the ark?

6. Who was the most successful physician in the Bible?

7. How do we know they used arithmetic in early Bible times?

8. How long did Cain hate his brother?

9. Who was the first electrician in the Bible?

10. Who sounded the first bell in the Bible?

p**i**c*k* t**h**e*s*e

Through the Goalposts

In the drawing on the right, an imaginary football goal post has been made using toothpicks. In the center of the goal post is a football. Your challenge is to see if you can turn the goal posts upside down and make the football land outside of the goal posts. You can only move two toothpicks to accomplish this trick. Can you do it? Once you have figured out how to do it, try the problem with a friend.

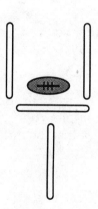

Double Sixes

In the drawing on the right, you will notice that six toothpicks are used to form a hexagon. See if you can add three more toothpicks to the six and form another regular six-sided figure. This one will really fool your friends.

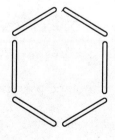

The Exploding Star

In the Star puzzle below you will notice that there are six small triangles made out of toothpicks and two large triangles made out of toothpicks that make up the star.

One day there was an explosion in the star and two of the toothpicks were blown into a new position. As a result of the explosion, the star was formed with six triangles rather than eight triangles. Which two toothpicks were blown into a new position?

Take eighteen toothpicks and form a star with them. See if you can figure out this explosive puzzle.

Nine To Five

Give your friend nine toothpicks. Ask him to take the toothpicks and challenge him to lay them out in such a way that the nine toothpicks form five triangles.

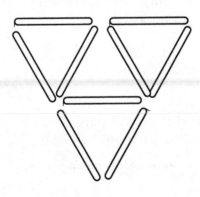

what's your angle?

Look at the illusion below. What angle can be seen but is not drawn?

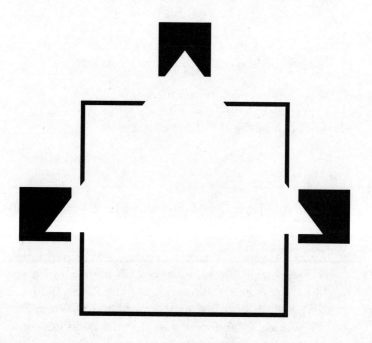

thought twisters

1. Mr. Cross and Mr. West each played seven sets of tennis. Mr. Cross won seven of the sets and Mr. West won seven of the sets. There were no ties. How could this be possible?

2. What three-letter word of one syllable changes to a three-syllable word by adding one letter?

3. Why is "H" good for deafness?

4. What can be right but never wrong?

5. If you shoot at four birds on a branch and kill one, how many will remain?

6. What five-letter word becomes shorter when you add two letters to it?

7. It was a typical fall day and many leaves had fallen to the ground. Mr. Lilley asked his eight children to rake up the leaves. They raked five piles in the back yard and three piles in the front yard. When Mr. Lilley and his children put the piles together, how many piles of leaves did they have?

8. Do you remember the story of King Midas? Every thing he touched turned to gold. One day he walked past three coils of rope 50 feet long and touched them. Instantly they turned into golden ropes. Wanting to view the beauty of the ropes and not wanting the ropes stolen by anyone, King Midas had his servants hang them in his royal palace. They were tied into three hooks in the ceiling behind his throne. The ropes hung one foot apart. The servants constructed a ladder to hang the golden ropes, after which the ladder was destroyed. The height of the hooks guaranteed sudden death if anyone tried to climb the golden ropes and slipped and fell. One evening a clever thief entered the king's throne room and stole all three ropes. He did not have any assistance or any way to get to the hooks other than climbing the golden ropes. The ropes were so high that he only had strength enough to climb one rope, one time. How did the thief get away with all three ropes without losing his life?

9. The following is a mighty fine problem. Can you, in four straight strokes of your pencil or pen, connect the dots below? You cannot lift your pencil or pen from the paper. And to make it harder, you cannot cross or retrace any line.

10. The arrows in the diagram below point the way to a very common English word. If you can solve the puzzle you will discover this familiar word.

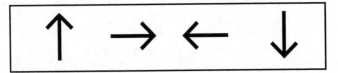

11. Try to figure out this cooking problem. You throw away the outside and cook only the inside. Then you will serve your food and eat only the outside and throw away the inside. What are you cooking and eating?

12. Which of the following choices is the best to say? "The yolk of the eggs *are* white" or "the yolk of the eggs *is* white?"

13. If you had a 1" by 12" wooden beam that was 12' long, how long would it take to cut 12 equal sections if it took one minute per section?

14. One day during the 1800s a cowboy rode into town. As he entered the town he saw two different men who were selling health elixir in a bottle. The men claimed that their elixir would cure any stomach ailment. One of the men was wearing a black hat and the other was wearing a white hat. The cowboy tied up his horse and went to the sheriff's office. He asked the sheriff if the two men were telling the truth. The sheriff said, "One of them fellas always lies."

The cowboy went up to the two men. He spoke to the man in the white hat and said, "Are you telling

the truth about your stomach elixir?" The man in
the black hat replied, "He'll say yes, but he will be
lying to you." Which man was the liar? The man in
the white hat or the man in the black hat?

15. In Fresno, California, you cannot take a picture of a
man with a wooden leg. Why not?

16. How far can a black bear run into the woods?

17. Match the opposite meaning with the numbered
words.

1. Relax _____	A.	Inadequate
2. Scarcity _____	B.	Reward
3. Declivity _____	C.	Clumsiness
4. Complete _____	D.	Select
5. Famous _____	E.	Power
6. Reject _____	F.	Tighten
7. Sufficient _____	G.	Plenty
8. Impotence _____	H.	Ascent
9. Penalize _____	I.	Idle
10. Secede _____	J.	Colorful
11. Vanish _____	K	Unknown
12. Drab _____	L.	Plain
13. Precipice _____	M.	Appear
14. Dexterity _____	N.	Join
15. Occupied _____	O.	Partial

w o r d q u i z # 3

See if you can solve these word puzzles.

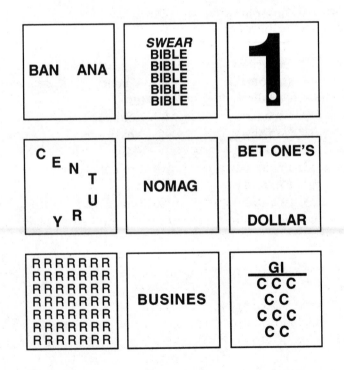

fantastic card tricks

Your First Card Trick

If you have never done a card trick before try this one out. It is very simple. You will need a regular deck of cards with the jokers removed.

Ask a friend to shuffle the deck of cards for you. Take the deck and fan it out face down. Have your friend select any card, pull it out, and memorize it. He can even show it to other people in the room.

While your friend is looking at his card, hold the rest of the deck in your right hand, face down. Split the deck of cards in half and look at the bottom card in your left hand. Don't let your friend see you looking. Be sure you memorize that card.

Then tell your friend to place his card face down on the deck of cards in your right hand. Be sure to place the other half of the deck in your left hand on top of his chosen card. In this way, you now have the card you memorized sitting on top of the card that your friend chose. Cut the deck a couple of times making sure you don't cut between those two cards.

Since you know that your memorized card is on top of (or in front of) the chosen card, you can now show your great showmanship in one of two ways (or you can come up with your own finale).

1. You can take the cards off the top of the deck one at a time and turn them over in front of your friend. When you come to the card you memorized you know that your friend's chosen card is next. You can say, "The next card that I turn over is your card." He will be amazed.

2. You can take the cards off the top of the deck one at a time and turn them over in front of your friend. Put them on the table so that you can see most of the faces of all of the cards. When you come to the card you memorized you know that your friend's chosen card is next. Turn your friend's chosen card over and drop it on the table with the rest of the cards. Pretend like you don't think that is the right card. You can make comments like, "I don't see it yet." Keep turning cards over until you only have five cards left in your hand. Make sure not to cover your friend's card on the table. Then look up at your friend and say, "The next card I turn over is going to be your card."

Your friend will think that he's got you. He knows that you have already dropped the chosen card on the table. He thinks you are going to turn over the next card in your hand. You then look down at the pile of cards on the table, grab the chosen card, and turn it over. This way you will give him a "double whammy" and fool him twice. He will sure be startled!

Great Magic

This is a tremendous card trick that is guaranteed to fool your friends. You will need a deck of 52 cards without jokers.

Have your friend shuffle the deck any way he would like. He can mix it up until he is satisfied. Then take the deck of cards and deal out three cards side by side on the table. Proceed from left to right adding a card to each of the three piles until there are seven cards in each pile for a total of 21 cards.

Ask your friend to point to one of the piles. It doesn't matter which pile he chooses. Pick up the pile he chose and fan out the cards so that you are looking at the back of the cards and your friend is looking at the face of the cards. Have your friend mentally select one of the cards and remember what is on it. Be sure to tell him not to touch any of the cards or tell you what is on it. Once the card has been mentally selected, fold up the chosen stack and place it on top of one of the other stacks. Place the remaining stack on top of the chosen stack.

Next, deal out the cards like you did in the beginning . . . three stacks . . . left to right . . . with seven cards in each stack. Pick up the first stack and fan the cards with the faces toward your friend. Ask your friend if the card he selected is in that stack. If he says yes, fold up the chosen stack and set it down on one of the other stacks. Then place the remaining stack on top of the chosen stack. If your friend says that his chosen card is not in the first stack go on to the second stack and do the same thing. If your friend indicates that the chosen card is not in the first two stacks then fan out the third stack. It doesn't matter which stack the chosen card is in. All that matters is that you place the chosen stack in the middle, between the other two stacks.

For the third time, deal out the cards in three stacks . . . left to right . . . for a total of seven cards in each stack. Again fan out each of the stacks until your friend indicates which stack his chosen card is in. Place the chosen stack on top of one of the other stacks and place the remaining stack on top of the chosen stack.

Now pick up all three stacks. Take the first card off the top of the deck and turn it over so that it is face up. As you do this, pronounce the letter "G." Take the next card off the top, turn it face up, and pronounce the letter "R." Keep doing this until you spell two words: G-R-E-A-T M-A-G-I-C. As soon as you have spelled out great magic . . . the next card to be turned over will be the one your friend chose. And he will be surprised and impressed by your great magic prowess.

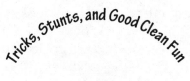

amazing

Your friends will be amazed by this super card trick. You need a regular deck of 52 cards and no jokers.

Tell your friend that you have great mental powers. Brag that you have the ability to know which card he will select out of a deck of cards. Let your friend know that your mental ability is so great that you will not even touch the cards!

Have your friend shuffle the deck until he is satisfied that it is mixed up. Next have him deal out three cards on the table side by side. Have him do the same thing again, placing a new card on top of each of the three stacks until there are five cards in each of the three stacks. Tell him to place the remaining cards on the table out of the way.

Tell your friend that he can select any one of the three stacks of cards. When he selects one of the stacks, have him look at the stack but not let you see the faces of the cards. Instruct him to mentally choose one of the cards and remember it. Ask him to be sure of what he has chosen. Then have him place the chosen stack on top of one of the other stacks. Next, have him place the remaining stack on top of the chosen stack.

Now, have your friend deal out three cards on the table again, placing one card on each of the three separate cards until there are five cards in each of the three stacks.

Have him select any one of the three stacks on the table. Tell him to fan the cards and look for his chosen card. If it is not in that stack, have him put those cards on the pile you set aside and go to the next stack. When he finally finds the stack with the chosen card you must watch very carefully. His chosen card will be the one in the middle of the stack. Remember, there are five cards left. His chosen card will be the third one.

Once your friend has identified the stack with his chosen card, have him place the stack face down on the table in front of him. Ask him to slowly separate the cards. Tell him this is to help you choose the right card with your great mental powers. You are looking for the third card (the middle card of the five cards). Have your friend move the cards apart from each other, but not in a straight line. Be sure to watch where he moves the third (middle) card.

Your friend will be looking at the back of five cards on the table. He knows that you have not seen any of the cards. He knows it is impossible for you to select the right card.

Tell your friend that you are beginning to get the mental image of which card he selected, but you need to eliminate some of the other cards. Have your friend select any card and point to it. If he points to the chosen card (the middle or third one), tell him to leave that one for now. . . . *You just aren't sure.* . . . Then have him select another card. When he does, say, "That is not your chosen card." Have him turn the card over and discard it. Keep doing this process of elimination until the only card remaining is the third or middle card.

Tell your friend to turn over the last card on the table. The shocked look on his face will be *amazing!*

Sensational

You will need a regular deck of 52 cards with no jokers for this sensational card trick. Ask your friend to shuffle the deck and cut it as close to halfway as he possibly can. To help do this, place the two cuts side by side for a visual check.

Have your friend select one of the two piles of cards. Instruct him to choose a card out of the middle of that stack and pull it out. Have him memorize the card and put it on top of the deck he selected, making sure you don't see what was selected. Then have him take the remaining pile and place it on top of those cards.

Next, have your friend deal out the entire deck into four piles. Have him deal from left to right starting with the top card. When finished, have him turn the four piles over so that the faces of the cards show.

Have your friend point at the pile that contains his chosen card without letting you know his specific card. Turn that pile over so you only see the backs of the cards. Discard the remaining three piles of cards.

Now, have your friend again deal out the remaining pile of cards into four stacks . . . from left to right . . . starting with the top card. He will have one card left. Have him place it on the first stack, and then discard that stack. That will leave three piles with three cards in each pile.

Now have your friend take the top and bottom cards away from each of the three stacks. That will leave the three middle cards remaining on the table. Have your friend discard the card on the right. Then have your friend remove the card on the left and discard it. That only leaves the middle card.

Look at your friend and say, "You are about to see a sensational mental demonstration. The card that you chose is remaining on the table. Turn it over." As he turns the card over, his mouth will drop open and he will wonder, "How did you do that?"

SWAT Team

Before you show this trick to your friend, you will need to do a little preparation. First, you will need a regular deck of 52 cards without jokers. Go through the deck of cards and pull out the four aces—they are your SWAT team. Spread the four aces out so that you can see all four cards side-by-side or vertically in your hand. Either direction will work. Next, take three other cards and place them behind the four aces and square them up. By doing this, your friend will not know they are there. The three other cards are now on top of the four aces. Don't turn the cards around or let your friend see the trick from the side.

You can say to your friend, "You see these four aces? They represent a police SWAT team. The police chief sends in the SWAT team when there is any trouble in town." Then, with your other hand, point to the table and the rest of the cards in the deck. "Those cards represent a hotel where there are some burglars. The police chief sent the SWAT team to the building by helicopter." At this point square up the four aces in your hand, along with the three other cards on top of them. Your friend will not notice that there are really seven cards in your hand.

Move your hand holding the four aces like it was a helicopter. Land on top of the deck of cards on the table. You can say, "The helicopter landed on top of the hotel and the four aces got out. The chief of police told one of them to go down to the basement to see if he could find the burglars. Take the top card off the deck and slide it in toward the bottom of the deck. Be sure that your friend does not see that it is not one of the aces. "The chief then told the second SWAT team member to go to the third floor and see if he could find any burglars." Take the second top card and put it about midway into the deck on the table. "The chief told the third SWAT team member to go to the fifth floor to see if he could find any burglars." Take the top card off the deck and put it about three-fourths of the way from the top. "And the other team member stayed on the top of the hotel as a lookout."

The SWAT team looked for the burglars but could not find them. They used their radios and contacted the team member on lookout duty. "We can't find anybody. The hotel is empty." The lookout radioed the chief to tell him the situation. "I know," said the chief, "the helicopter pilot dropped you on the wrong hotel. Get your men back to the top of the hotel. The helicopter is going to pick you up in a few minutes." The lookout radioed the other SWAT team members to come to the roof. They ran as fast as they could up the stairs. (Tap the top of the deck of cards a few times like someone running up the stairs).

"In about a minute the four SWAT team members were together again at the top of the hotel." As you say that, begin to turn over the top four cards and lay them on the table. It will look like the four aces rose through the deck.

When your friend asks you to do the trick again say, "I would but the SWAT team has to go to another hotel and look for more burglars."

building blocks

How many building blocks do you see?

Are there six or seven blocks?

Are you looking down on the blocks or are you looking up?

Try to work your way through this building-block maze.

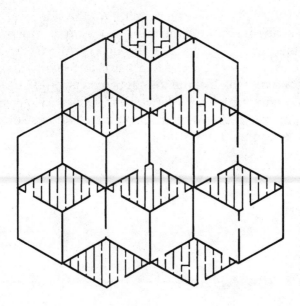

crazy pictures
quiz #3

Do you think you can identify the pictures below? Give it a shot!

bible riddles #5

1. How did Jonah feel when the great fish swallowed him?
2. Why are a pair of roller skates like the forbidden fruit in the Garden of Eden?
3. What does the story of Jonah and the great fish teach us?
4. Do you know how you can tell that David was older than Goliath?
5. What is the difference between Noah's ark and an archbishop?
6. When did Ruth treat Boaz badly?
7. Where was Solomon's temple located?
8. Who is the fastest runner in the world?
9. If Moses were alive today why would he be considered a remarkable man?
10. How do we know that Noah had a pig in the ark?

party tricks

The Reappearing Quarter

This is a great party trick. It's best to do this trick when you are wearing short sleeves. Tell your friends that you have learned a fantastic new magic trick. Take a quarter and place it in your hand. Let the group examine both of your hands. Place a cloth napkin or a handkerchief over the coin. Have different people in the group feel under the napkin to see that the coin is still in the palm of your hand.

Walk to the center of the room and slowly pull the napkin off of your hand. The coin will be gone. Hand the napkin to your friends and let them examine it. They will be amazed.

Next, let everyone examine your hands again and the napkin. Place the napkin over the palm of your hand. Walk around and let several people reach under the napkin to be sure that there is no coin there.

Walk to the center of the room and slowly pull the napkin off of your hand. The quarter will have reappeared. Do not repeat the trick.

The secret lies in the fact that you have an accomplice. The first time you walked around the room, people felt under the napkin to see if the coin was there. The last person to feel under the napkin is your accomplice. He will take the coin off of the palm of your hand and hold it. When he removes his hand, he will say, "It's still there." When you take the napkin off the coin will be gone. Of course it will, your accomplice has it!

When you come around the room the second time, people will feel under the napkin to be sure that there is no coin in your palm. The last person to feel under the napkin will be your friend. He will put the quarter in your hand, pull out his hand from under the napkin, and say, "There is no coin there."

Pirate Treasure

Tell your friends that you have the power to identify "pirate treasure." Your friends will be the pirates; the treasure will be one of three objects chosen by the group.

You will leave the room. The "pirates" will place three objects on the floor or table in front of them. They will choose one of the objects to be the treasure. Have them call you back into the room to see if you can identify which object belongs in the treasure chest. You will always be able to identify the "pirate treasure."

The secret of this trick lies in the fact that you have a silent partner in the group of pirates. Your partner will give away the secret by using his thumbs. Your partner will fold his hands in front of him. If his right thumb is over his left thumb, the object chosen will be on the right. (Be sure to agree ahead of time that it is your *partner's right* you are talking about). If his left thumb is over his right thumb, the object chosen is at your partner's left. If your partner's thumbs are side by side and not crossing, the object chosen will be in the center.

Cahoots

Explain to the group at the party that you and your friend are mental wizards. Your minds are so great that you can think each other's thoughts. And all you have to do is concentrate deeply until your minds meld and you are in cahoots. Cahoots means to blend together and work together in collaboration. (It is always good to ask at the beginning of any party game if anyone has played it before. If some people say they have, ask them to not reveal the secret to the rest of the group.)

You begin this stunt by having your accomplice leave the room. Then have the group select a person or an object in the room to be identified by your accomplice when she returns. Next, pick up a broom or a yardstick to use as a pointer, and something to draw with on the ground.

When the group has selected a person have your accomplice reenter the room. You will both look at each other. At one point you will say to your accomplice, "Are we in cahoots?" She will say either yes or no. As soon as she says yes begin to draw little crazy drawings on the ground with the broom handle or yard stick. Then point to different objects and people in the room with your broomstick or yardstick. As you point to different objects or people your accomplice will say no—until you are pointing to the person or object chosen. Your friends will be baffled. They won't be able to figure out what you are doing. You can demonstrate this trick a number of times without them discovering your secret.

The secret to cahoots is very simple. When your accomplice enters the room you will look at each other silently for a moment. During that moment both of you will be concentrating. You are listening for some obvious movement, noise, or comment by someone in the group. Someone will always do something: cough, move, snicker, or make some off-the-wall comment. As soon as an obvious noise, movement, or comment has been made you say, "Are we in cahoots?" If your accomplice has noticed the same movement or comments she will say yes. If she is not sure, she will say no. Then become silent again until someone in the crowd makes a disturbance that you both notice.

Once you are in cahoots take your yardstick or broomstick and begin to draw on the floor. You can make circles, draw lines, tap, and point at meaningless objects in the room. All of these movements are just an act to confuse and fool the crowd. They have nothing to do with the secret of the trick.

When you finally point to the individual that has made the noise, comment, or disturbance, your accomplice will know that *the very next thing you point at is the chosen person or object.*

After the crowd has been sufficiently impressed have your friend leave the room and demonstrate the trick again. After several times switch places: you leave the room and your accomplice takes your place. This will fool the people even more.

You can do this trick six or seven times. After that the group might get discouraged. Make sure you quit while their interest is high. Be sure not to reveal your secret. That's what makes this trick so much fun. Let the group try and figure it out.

tricky fun

The Money-Maker

Turn to your friend and say, "I have learned the secret of making money. Let me show you."

Take five quarters and ask your friend to hold them. Reach over and grab a nearby magazine. Slightly fold the magazine so that both sides are bending up. Ask your friend to place the quarters in the slightly folded magazine. Ask him how many quarters he put into the magazine.

"Five."

"Correct."

Now say, "I have found the secret of making money. It's dill pickles. All you do is take a magazine like this and put your money into the fold. Then you say 'dill pickles,' and your money will multiply. Let me show you. Hold out your hands.

"*Dill pickles.*" As you say dill pickles, tip the magazine up so that the quarters pour into your friend's hand. Then ask him to count the quarters. He will have ten quarters in his hand.

Of course you know that you prepared the magazine ahead of time. You secretly hid five quarters in the pages of the magazine. So when you tipped the magazine up, the five quarters poured into your friend's hands. They were joined by the five quarters hidden in the pages. You can use pennies, nickels, or dimes if you wish.

How to Make a Little Scratch

You will need a glass, two quarters, a dime, and a table with a tablecloth on it. Place the dime on the tablecloth. Next place one quarter on either side of the dime. Then turn the glass over, resting it on top of the two quarters.

Challenge your friend to remove the dime without touching the glass, without touching the quarters, and without touching the dime or blowing on it.

After he gives up, say to your friend that you bet that you can get the dime out from under the glass, without touching the glass without touching the quarters, without touching the dime or blowing on it. Your friend won't believe you! But you can prove him wrong.

Place four fingers on the tablecloth in front of the glass. Be sure not to touch the glass. Begin to scratch the tablecloth with all four fingers at the same time. It won't be long until the dime will come walking out from under the glass without you touching it!

The Perfect Cut

Take a piece of string about two feet long. Tie one end to a cup and the other end to a doorknob. Let the cup hang on the string that is tied to the doorknob.

Hand your friend a pair of scissors and tell her to cut the string so that the cup will not hit the ground. Tell her that she cannot catch the cup or prop something under it. It must be hanging.

After she gives up, go to the string. Grab it in the middle. Make a loop and a knot in the string. When you finish, the cup should still be hanging on the string except now there is a loop tied in the string.

Take the scissors and cut the middle of the loop. You have cut the string but the cup didn't drop to the ground.

The Special Name

Take a sheet of paper and fold it in a letter fold with three separate sections. Take the paper that is letter folded and divide it vertically into thirds by folding in the right and left sides. Tear the paper down the folds until you have nine different pieces approximately the same size. Place the nine pieces of paper into a hat or bowl. Then draw out one piece of paper and hand it to your friend. Have him write a special name on that piece of paper, and fold it in half. Next hand him the eight remaining pieces of paper and have him write eight different names on the pieces then fold them in half.

Have your friend drop all nine pieces into a hat or bowl and mix them up. Then tell him that you're sure you can tell which name was the special one. You will pull the pieces out of the hat one by one, read the name, and place the paper on the table in random order.

After reading all the names, reach forward and pick up the piece of paper with the special name and read it to your friend. He will be flabbergasted!

The trick? After you rip the paper into nine squares, pick up the pieces and drop them in a hat. But make sure that the last piece of paper you pick up and put into the hat is the one in the center. Then reach into the hat and *pull out the center piece of paper first*. Have your friend write the *special name* on that piece.

The center piece with the *special name* on it will be easy to identify. It will be the piece of paper with ripped edges on all four sides. Your friend won't be able to figure this one out.

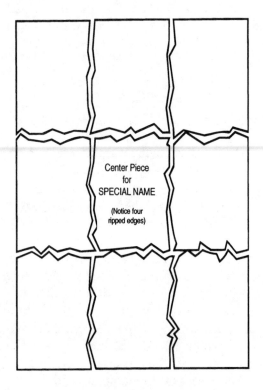

Center Piece
for
SPECIAL NAME

(Notice four
ripped edges)

The Unpopable Balloon

Take an ordinary balloon and blow it up. Tie a knot in the end so the air won't go out. Place a piece of cellophane tape on one side of the balloon.

Then take the balloon and a straight pin to your friend. Say, I can poke this balloon with a pin and it will not pop." They will probably say, "Yeah, right. Prove it."

Be sure to hold the side of the balloon with the cellophane tape toward you. Take the pin and poke it through the tape. The balloon will not pop—even if you do it a couple of times.

Next, hand the pin to one of your friends and say, "Here, you try it." Be sure that you hold on to the balloon with both hands with the cellophane tape still facing you.

When your friend sticks the pin in the balloon it will pop. Chances are your friends will not examine the pieces after it pops. You will have had a "popping good time" and your friends will be really impressed.

Filled to the Brim

Get a glass of water and fill it to the brim. Ask your friend, "Do you think I can get anything else in this glass?" He will probably say, "Nope. It would spill over the edge."

Respond by saying, "I'll bet I can!" Then begin to drop straight pins into the water. You can get lots of pins in the water before it spills over the edge!

Salt and Pepper

Take a saucer and sprinkle salt onto it. Then sprinkle some pepper on top of the salt. Hand the saucer to your friend and say, "Can you separate the salt from the pepper without touching either the salt or the pepper?" Your friend will look at the saucer and say, "No one can do that." But you just simply smile and say, "Ah, but I can."

Take out a plastic pen and a piece of felt or wool that you have hidden in your pocket. Rub the pen very hard and fast with the felt or wool. Then slowly wave the pen over the saucer. The pepper will be attracted to the pen by static electricity.

Be careful not to get too close to the saucer. Pepper is lighter than salt and will rise first, but if you get too close to the salt your pen will also pick up the salt. Be sure to practice this a few times before you show it to your friend.

flip flop

As you study the illusions below they will flip-flop right before your very eyes!

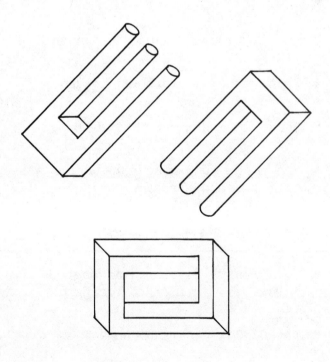

83

bible riddles #6

1. Why did Moses cross the Red Sea?

2. Who was the most popular actor in the Bible?

3. Who was the most ambitious man in the Bible?

4. Who were the first twin boys in the Bible?

5. Where is baseball mentioned in the Bible?

6. Who was the first person in the Bible to eat herself out of house and home?

7. Why was Job always cold in bed?

8. Where were the Egyptians paid for goods taken by the Israelites when they fled from Egypt?

9. Why didn't they play cards on Noah's ark?

pranks

I Beg Your Pardon

This is a fun trick to do if you are wearing a coat. (It can also be done in the front pocket of your pants.)

Take your coat and put a spool of thread into the inside pocket. If you have a dark coat, use light thread; if you have a light coat, use dark thread. Take a needle and pull the thread through the fabric of the coat. Leave enough thread sticking out so that it is quite noticeable. Remove the needle and have lots of fun.

Your friends will come up and see the thread and they'll want to do you a favor by taking it off your coat. Be sure to act like you have no idea the thread is there. When they grab the thread and start to toss it away, it will get longer and longer. It will look as if they are unraveling your coat. Your friends will be shocked and embarrassed.

You can have many good laughs with this one. Be sure to keep the needle with you so you can set up the trick again if the thread gets pulled back into your coat. You will be able to do this trick many times before the day is over.

A Special Calendar

Ask your friend, "Which month has 28 days in it?"
He will probably answer, "February."
Smile and say, "Actually, every month has 28 days in it."

Spelling Bee

Ask your friends to help you spell some words.
When they agree you're all set–
"How do you spell the word joke?"
"J–O–K–E."
"How do you spell the word folk?"
"F–O–L–K."
"How do you spell the word poke?"
"P–O–K–E."
"How do you spell the white of an egg?"
"Y–O–L–K."
"No, that is the yellow part of an egg. The white of an egg is called 'albumen.' "

Total Black Out

Ask your friend to help you with a math problem. Ask him to add 6 and 6 together. Next, have him subtract 3 from his answer. Then have him add 1 to that answer. Finally, have him subtract five from that answer.

Now, tell your friend to close his eyes and concentrate on his answer. Then say (while their eyes are closed), "Dark isn't it?"

Shock a Parent

If your mother or father is in the habit of coming into your room to wake you up in the morning you can have fun with this one.

Get up a little earlier than usual and get dressed for school. Then crawl back into bed and pretend you are asleep. Pull the covers up enough so no one can tell that you are already dressed.

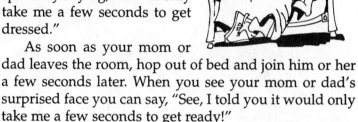

When he or she comes in and says, "It's time to get up, you're going to be late," Respond by saying, "It will only take me a few seconds to get dressed."

As soon as your mom or dad leaves the room, hop out of bed and join him or her a few seconds later. When you see your mom or dad's surprised face you can say, "See, I told you it would only take me a few seconds to get ready!"

An Arm-Twister

Challenge your friend: "I bet you can't put your right hand where your left hand can't reach it."

He will probably say, "I'll bet I can."

Then say, "Okay, put your right hand on your left elbow."

Sawdust

Ask your friend to help you with a math problem. Have her add up the following items and see how many tons she comes up with.

> One ton of sawdust.
> Three tons of smelly shoes.
> Two tons of nuts and bolts.
> Three tons of bubble gum.
> One ton of fat.

Ask your friend, "Do you have all of that in your head?"

"Yes."

Then you say, "I thought so!"

Pillow Talk

This prank has been around for years. Balance a pillow on a door that is slightly open. When a person enters the room the pillow will fall on his head. The pillow won't hurt him but he will know he's been had.

Follow Directions

Hand your friend a pencil and a piece of paper. Ask him to write a small (lower case) "I" with a dot over it.

He will probably write "i".

Say, "I'm sorry, but a lower case 'i' with a dot over it is written like this:

．

i

Mind Over Matter

Inform your friend that you are a great mind reader. Hand him a piece of paper and a pen and ask him to write any word, quote, or phrase on it. You can look away and say, "Tell me when you are ready." Tell him not to tell you what he is writing. Then have him fold the paper a couple of times.

After he has written on the paper and folded it, tell him to place it on the floor and stand on it—you want to make this feat as difficult as possible.

Look at your friend and ask, "Do you think I will be able to tell you what is on that piece of paper you just wrote?" He will probably say, "No way."

Then act as if you are in deep concentration: "Hmm . . . it's coming to me. What's on the paper? What's on the paper?" Look troubled as if you are having a hard time. "I've got it! *You* are on the paper."

Money Flies Away

Take an envelope and write the following on the outside of it:

Inside is my gift to you.
It is a ten dollar bill.
Please do not ever open this envelope . . .

Next take a 3 x 5 card and write the following:

. . . or the ten dollar bill
will vanish!

Place it inside the envelope and put the envelope in a conspicuous place where your friend will find it.

word quiz #4

See if you can identify these word puzzles.

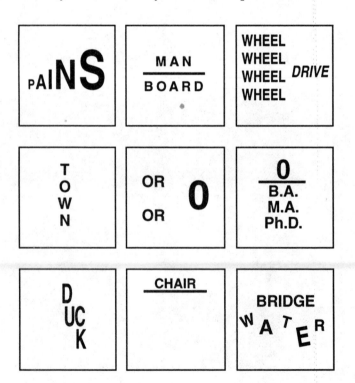

brain-benders

See if you can identify the pictures below.

Tricks, Stunts, and Good Clean Fun

wild stunts

Toe-Jumping Contest

Place a pencil on the floor in front of your feet so that your toes almost touch it. Bend over and grasp the front of your toes.

Now, jump over the pencil without releasing your hold on your toes. With practice you will be able to jump a fair distance. With more practice you can even jump backwards.

After you have mastered "toe jumping," challenge your friends to a contest to see who can jump the farthest.

Crisscross Dip

Can you do this balance challenge? Place a sheet of music, paper, or cardboard on the floor in front of you. Fold the piece of paper or cardboard so it stands upright. Stand with both of your toes on a line.

Grasp your right ear with your left hand. Bend your right leg behind your left knee and grab your right foot by bringing your arm in front of your body and holding on with your right hand. Try it a couple of times.

Now bend your left leg a little and lean your body forward. Without letting go of your ear or foot, bend forward and pick up the cardboard with your teeth . . . without losing your balance. Once you have this mastered try switching ears and toes.

Slap/Clap

The object of this stunt is to see who can make the other person move their feet first. First you and a friend should stand facing each other. Each of you should have your feet pressed together.

Now both of you will hold your hands in front of you and try to slap/clap each other's hands. You can use one or both hands at the same time. You can also draw the other person off-guard by pretending to slap/clap his hands but stopping short. This may cause the other person to come forward too far, lose his balance, and move his feet. It is also possible that both of you will slap/clap at the same time and knock each other backward causing both of you to move your feet at the same time.

Play this stunt with your friend a number of times. The person who moves his feet the least is the winner. This also would be great fun at a party where you could make it a contest with "elimination" rounds.

Lead Foot

Tell your friend that you have some invisible lead and that you can put the lead on his foot so he won't be able to lift that foot up.

Your friend will want to see this stunt. Have him stand against a wall with his left or right side pressed against the wall. His shoulder, hip, thigh, knee, and one

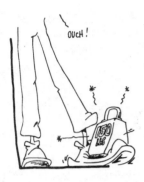

foot should all be touching the wall. His other foot should be about a foot away from the wall.

Place the imaginary lead on your friend's foot that is away from the wall. Then ask your friend to lift the foot with the lead on it. He won't be able to do it! In fact, it can't be done—even without your imaginary lead.

World's Strongest Thumb

Are you ready to show off your great strength? This is how to do it! Say to your friend, "I'm sure you've heard of Hercules, Atlas, Mr. Universe, and other strong people. Today, I would like to show you the "world's strongest thumb." As you say this, hold up and admire your thumb. Then continue: "I'll give you a demonstration."

Have your friend sit in a chair and look back and up at the ceiling. Place your thumb on his or her forehead. Then ask your friend to get up out of the chair without using his or her hands. You will be able to hold him or her in the chair by only using *"the world's strongest thumb."*

squeeze play

Study the illusion below. Are the lines of the diamond straight or do they bend?

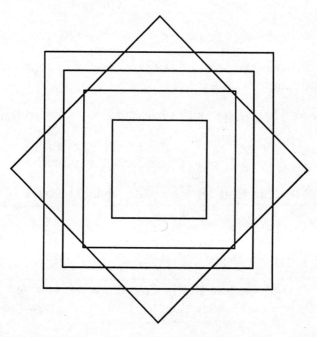

bible riddles #7

1. Who was the straightest man in the Bible?

2. Which came first—the chicken or the egg?

3. When is high finance first mentioned in the Bible?

4. What is the only wage that does not have any deductions?

5. At what season of the year did Eve eat the fruit?

6. If Methuselah was the oldest man in the Bible (969 years of age), why did he die before his father?

7. What has God never seen, Abraham Lincoln seldom saw, and we see every day?

8. On the ark, Noah probably got milk from the cows. What did he get from the ducks?

9. One of the first things Cain did after he killed his brother was to take a nap. How do we know this?

10. Where do you think the Israelites may have deposited their money?

Tricks, Stunts, and Good Clean Fun

more flimflam

Hit the Table

Take a coin and place it on the table in front of you. Ask your friend if he can take a second coin and put it under the first coin without touching the coin on the table. You can inform him that it is okay to hit the top of the table.

After he hits the top of the table for a while he will finally give up. Then inform your friend that you can place the second coin under the first coin without touching it. Your friend will say, "I don't think so—prove it!"

Take the second coin in one hand. Lightly hit the top of the table with the other hand. (This is just for effect.) Then take the hand with the coin and place it under the table. Now turn to your friend and say, "I have now put the second coin under the first coin without touching it."

The Big Push

All you will need for this bit of fun is a ring on your finger, an object larger than the ring, and a stiff object that will fit through your ring. This trick can be done almost anywhere and is guaranteed to fool anyone.

Take the ring off your finger. Locate a larger object — it could be a salt shaker, glass, book, or shoe.

Tell your friend that you can push (the object) through your ring. Let's use a salt shaker as an example. It is larger than the hole in your ring. Your friend will look at the salt shaker and the hole in your ring and will say that it is impossible.

You simply look at him and say, "I bet that I can push this salt shaker through my ring." Your friend will probably say, "I'll bet you can't."

Take your ring and hold it between your first finger and your thumb in front of the medium-sized object. Next (and here comes the trick) take a pen, a knife, a straw, or any stiff object smaller than the hole in your ring. Push the small object (a straw for example) through the hole in your ring and keep pushing until it pushes the salt shaker. You have now pushed the salt shaker through your ring. Your friend will scream, "Unfair!" But you have done exactly what you said you were going to do.

Kitchen Craziness

This is a good trick that can be done at home in your own kitchen. When you and your friends are in the kitchen, turn to them and say, "I'll bet you that I can carry water in a facial tissue." With that, open the cupboard, take out a glass, and fill it with some water out of the faucet. Set the glass next to a facial tissue that you previously put on the table (or you can pull a new facial tissue out of a box or package).

Your friends will most likely ask, "You mean that you are going to take the water from that glass and carry it in a facial tissue? You're probably going to wrap the tissue around the glass and pick it up."

Basically you ignore whatever your friends say and restate what you are going to do. You say, "I am going to take this piece of facial tissue and I am going to carry water in it. The water will not be in any type of glass or container. The water will come in direct contact with this facial tissue and I will carry it around the room." Your friends will most likely say, "No way."

Pick up the glass of water on the table and take a drink. This has nothing to do with the trick other than to fool your friends more. Next, stand up and go over to the freezer. Open the door and pull out an ice cube you've set aside. Put it in the facial tissue and carry it around the room with a big smile. Be prepared to run for your life after this one.

Give Me a Break

Inform your friend that you have great magical powers. Tell your friend that you need three coins to demonstrate your ability. After he hands you three coins, ask him to carefully study and remember them. He can mark them with a pen or pencil or remember the dates on the coins.

Next, switch the coins from hand to hand in front of him. Every now and then stop and have him look at the coins to see if they are the same ones. Ask, "Are these the three coins you gave me?" Your friend will say that they are the same coins.

Next, put the coins behind your back and pretend you are doing something with them. Put two coins in one hand and one coin in the other. Now bring your hands from behind your back and open them. Ask your friend, "Are these the coins you gave me?" He will say yes. Look very surprised. Act as if something has gone wrong with your trick.

Ask again, "Are you positive that these are the three coins you gave me?" He will probably say, "I'm positive."

Then say, "If you are positive that these are the three coins you gave me, I want to say thanks for the gift." Put the three coins in your pocket. You may have to give back the coins or lose your life, but you will have had some fun.

A Fast Buck

Take a dollar bill and hold it at one end with your thumb and first finger. Let the rest of the bill hang down toward the ground.

Have your friend put his thumb and first finger around the dollar bill with his thumb right in front of the picture of Washington. His finger and thumb *should not* be touching the dollar bill.

Tell your friend that you will give him the dollar bill if he can catch it with his thumb and first finger. The only rule is that he may not move his hand down while the bill is falling. Let him try to catch it a few times as you drop it. Remember, the hand is quicker than the eye. The time it takes for your friend to see the bill drop from your hand and then react is too short for him to accomplish this impossible task.

An Outstanding Trick

Tell your friend that you know he is very strong but you have a feat that you don't think he is strong enough to perform. He will ask you what it is.

You say, "Okay. I'll bet you that I can put a piece of paper on the floor and you can put your toes on one edge and my toes will be on the other edge and you will not be able to push me off the paper.

He will probably respond by saying, "I'll bet I can."

After the challenge is accepted, go over to a doorway and set the piece of paper on the ground. Close the door so that you are on one side of the door and your friend is on the other side. Tell him to go ahead and try to push you off the paper.

Be sure *you* are standing on the outside of a door that opens inward. Your friend has to be on the side of the door that opens toward him or he may open the door and shove you off of the paper—and you will lose.

You're All Wet

Ask your friend if he thinks he can pour a glass of water down his neck without getting wet. If he says yes, ask him to demonstrate it for you. (He may figure out the trick.) If he does it correctly, congratulate them.

If he says no, you say, "I can pour a glass of water down my neck and not get wet!" After he says, "I'll bet you can't," take a glass of water and drink it.

A "Get In To" Trick

This trick will work with a number of different objects. You can use a glass, a cup, a wastepaper basket, or a vase.

Tell your friend that you can crawl into the object (for example, a salt shaker) with your entire body.

Your friend will say it's impossible and challenge you to do it. Simply smile and say, "*I can* do it."

Set the salt shaker (glass, vase, etc.) on the floor. Tell your friend that this feat takes a little preparation and you must leave the room for a moment but you will be right back.

101

When you get outside of the room get down on your hands and knees. Then crawl into the room, *in* to the salt shaker. As you are crawling say, "See, I was outside of the room and now I am crawling *in* to the salt shaker."

Across the Street

Turn to your friend and say, "I'll bet I can cross the street with one jump."

Your friend will probably say, "No one can do that."

You respond by saying, "I'm sure I can."

All you do is simply walk across the street and then take one jump. Turn to your friend and say, "Hey, I crossed the street with only one jump!"

Through the Keyhole

This is a great trick if you can find a door that has an old-fashioned keyhole in it. Tell your friend, "I can push myself through a keyhole." He will most likely say, "No way." Just smile and say, "watch."

Take a piece of paper and write the word *myself* on it. Roll it up and shove *"myself"* through the keyhole.

If you cannot find a keyhole use something else small like a ring, a coat hanger, or a bracelet.

Brain Waves

Take a nickel and stand it on end. Next, take a slender piece of paper about 1½ inches long and ¼ inches wide and balance it on top of the coin (see illustration). Finally, place a thin-walled glass over the paper and coin. Try and make sure that the piece of paper is close to the glass but not touching it.

Tell your friend that you have powerful brain waves. They are so powerful that you can make the paper on the coin move without touching the table, glass, coin, or paper. You will use only your brain waves.

Your friend will probably comment, "Your brain has just died. You can't do that."

You just smile.

Tell your friend that you need to activate your brain waves. Take out your comb and comb your hair a few times. Then bring the comb close to the glass. Be sure not to touch the glass. The static electricity from your hair should be enough to make the piece of paper move (and maybe even fall off the coin).

Four Coins in a Row

Take six coins and place them on a table in the form of a cross. Then challenge your friend to see if he can rearrange the six coins and get four coins in each row.

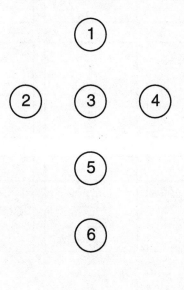

wor∂ quiz #5

Can you figure out these word puzzles?

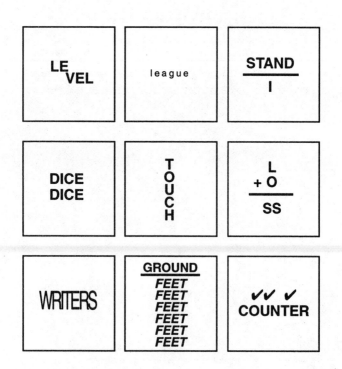

crazy picture
quiz #4

Can you guess what the pictures below mean?

105

min𝛿 warpers

1. There are different ways to travel from one place to another. What mode of conveyance has eight wheels but room for only one passenger?

2. Old MacDonald had a farm. And on that farm he had some horses. He had 7 brown horses, 5 black horses, 3 golden horses, 9 white horses, and 13 pinto horses. How many of Old MacDonald's horses can say they are the same color as another horse on the farm?

3. A big game hunter was out hunting in the jungle when he viewed a very strange event. He saw two snakes of the same size start to eat each other. Both snakes swallowed the tail of the other snake. The circle created by the snakes began to grow smaller and smaller as each kept eating the other. What do you suppose eventually happened?

4. An old farmer was walking down a road with a sack of lettuce, a fox, and a rabbit. Soon he came to a river that needed to be crossed. Because of a recent storm the old farmer could not wade across the river. It

was too deep. He looked around and found a log that was big enough for just him and the lettuce or him and the fox or him and the rabbit. He wanted to get all of his cargo over to the other side but he had a problem. If he took the lettuce across, the fox might eat the rabbit. If he took the fox across the rabbit might eat the lettuce. How did he solve the problem?

5. What letter is exactly in the middle of the alphabet?

6. Test your knowledge of sports. Swimmers wear nothing on their feet. Tennis players wear tennis shoes. Baseball and football players wear shoes with cleats. In what sport are the shoes made entirely of metal.

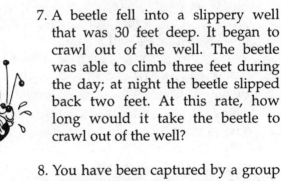

7. A beetle fell into a slippery well that was 30 feet deep. It began to crawl out of the well. The beetle was able to climb three feet during the day; at night the beetle slipped back two feet. At this rate, how long would it take the beetle to crawl out of the well?

8. You have been captured by a group of pirates. They inform you that they will feed you to the sharks unless you can correctly answer their tricky question: A rope ladder hangs over the side of the pirate ship moored to

the dock. The ladder has 20 rungs, spaced 8 inches apart. The bottom rung is just barely touching the water. The life determining question is, "If the tide rises at the rate of 12 inches an hour, how many rungs of the ladder will be covered by water in 90 minutes?"

9. An old rancher knew that he was about to die. He had three sons and wanted to leave his horses to them. He wrote out his will and left his oldest son half of the horses. To his second son he left one-third of the horses. To his youngest son he left one-ninth of the horses.

   After the old rancher died a problem arose. The three sons discovered that there were 17 horses. They couldn't figure out how to divide the horses like their father's will suggested. Finally they went to old Pete, the ranch foreman, and asked for his assistance. The grizzled old foreman said, "Shucks, that's an easy one." How did old Pete solve the problem?

10. Put on your thinking cap and try to come up with a five-letter word that has four personal pronouns in it.

11. What strange word in the English language contains three consecutive letters with dots over them?

12. Mr. Weston wanted to travel from his home in Reedley to the lake where he liked to fish. On the trip to the lake, it took him an hour-and-a-quarter to get there. When he drove back home, it took him 75 minutes. How could this be?

13. One day a king announced to his subjects that he would give his daughter's hand in marriage to any man who could master a very dangerous problem. Each man had to walk across a beam carrying three lead weights. The beam would be designed in such a way that it would carry the weight of the man with his clothes on plus two pounds. Each lead weight weighed one pound. If the beam broke the man would fall into a pit filled with alligators. Many men tried and failed because of the extra pound of weight. Finally, one young man was successful and won the king's daughter's hand in marriage. What was his secret?

14. In the rest of this mind warper, see if you can find three mistaks. Don't be foled: Be sure you look very carefully.

15. How well do you know your money? George Washington is pictured on the one-dollar bill. Abraham Lincoln is on the five-dollar bill. Which president is on the ten-dollar bill?

16. Many workers feel just like the following phrase. What does it mean?

17. There is a very strange word in the English language. It begins with the letters u–n–d and it ends with the letters u–n–d. What is this unusual word?

the puzzling pyramids

In the drawing below, see how many puzzling pyramids you can find. If you can find the correct number in less than one minute you are the champ.

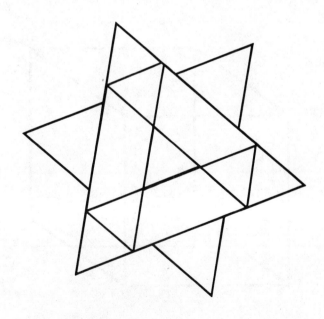

double vision

Carefully study the box below. As you do, it will change directions before your eyes.

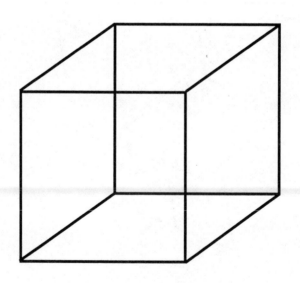

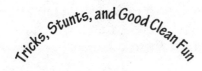

tan*t*ali*z*i**n**g tr*i*c*k*s

Math Magic

Take a piece of paper and an envelope. Write the number 1,089 on the paper and seal it in the envelope. Now you are ready for the trick.

Tell your friends that you are a math genius. Have them pick any three digit number* and give the following instuctions:

Example:

1. Write down the number selected   459
2. Reverse the number   954
3. Subtract the smaller number   -459
   from the larger number   495
4. Reverse the answer   594
5. Total the last two numbers   **1,089**

---

* The only three digit numbers this trick will not work for are numbers that are written the same backward or forward, such as: 141, 282, 363. If they select one of those numbers have them select another number. (They will think it is part of the trick.)

Once they get their answer (1,089) tell them what a math whiz you are. You knew what number they would select before they wrote it down. Of course they won't believe you. Hand them the envelope and tell them to look inside.

They won't believe their eyes.

Pick Up Sticks

This is a fun trick to do at a restaurant. Take five straws and put them in front of your friend. Tell him to try to take one of the straws and pick up the other four straws with it. Tell him that he cannot bend the ends or shove the straws inside of each other.

After he struggles with this one for a little while he will give up—then you show him how to do it. Take two of the straws and put them parallel to each other on the table. Next, take two more straws and form an X (diagonal lines) and lay them on top of the two parallel straws. Finally, weave the fifth straw under one of the parallel straws, over the top of the center of the X and back under the other parallel straw. You will now be able to pick up all five straws with one straw.

The Weight-Lifter Straw

Take a bottle and a straw and hand it to your friend. Ask him to pick up the bottle using only the straw. Tell him he cannot tie the straw around the neck of the bottle.

After he struggles a while and then gives up, show him how it is done. Take the straw and bend about 2 1/2 inches of it upward forming a V. One side of the V will be longer. Push the point of the V into the bottle until the 2 1/2 inch part of the straw begins to open up a little. Slowly pull on the longer side of the

V of the straw and you will be able to pick up the bottle using only a straw.

Triple Trouble

Take a 3 by 5 card or a piece of paper about the same size. Make two tears in the card all the way to about $1/2$" from the long edge (see illustration). The tears should make three pieces of about the same size.

Bet your friend that he will not be able to continue the tears so that the center piece will drop to the ground with one pull. Let him try.

Then get another card and rip it in the same manner. Say to your friend, "I'll bet that I can make the center piece fall to the ground with one pull."

Pick the card up. Quickly bite the center section with

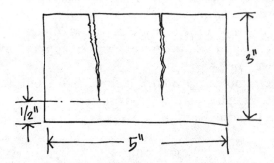

your teeth and do not let go. At the same time, pull the outer pieces apart. Then open your teeth and the center piece will fall to the ground.

Fruit Under Glass

If you live in an area where they grow fruit you can have fun with this trick. Find some clear bottles with a short neck. A milk bottle works perfectly for this fun fooler.

Let's say that you live where they grow apples or oranges. Take the bottle and tie a strong string around it. Put the bottle over an apple or orange when it first starts growing. The fruit will have to be small enough to fit into the bottle. Next, tie the bottle to the branch. The sun will do the rest.

The apple or orange (or almost any fruit) will begin to grow larger and larger in the bottle. It will continue to grow until it reaches its normal size and color. The clear glass allows the sun to color the fruit.

When the fruit is full grown and ripe, untie the string, cut the stem and the fruit will be fully grown inside the bottle. You can tell your friends that you wanted to save some canning time. You have developed a tree that grows both bottles and fruit together. Or you can challenge them to figure out how you got the fruit in the bottle! If you are in school, you can take it to show and tell and blow away your friends.

Double Your Money

Take two coins and put them on the table in front of you. Hold a pencil or pen upright between the coins. Make sure the point is half-way between the two coins.

Now stare at the point of the pencil. Slowly move the pencil toward you. Keep looking at the point as you bring it forward. As the pencil gets closer it will look like there are four coins on the table. You have doubled your money.

stunts

Windbag

If you want to have some fun with your friends try the windbag trick on them. Take a large book (such as a dictionary) and place it on the table. Open the pages of the book so that it will stand up by itself.

Challenge your friends to see if they can blow the book over with their breath. They will try and try but will not be able to do it. You then turn to them and say, "You know, I can blow the book over with my breath." Be prepared for rude remarks like, "Your breath would blow anything over." They will, of course, say that you won't be able to do it. You respond by saying, "I'll bet I can."

After they have accepted your challenge, take a paper bag and put it under the opened dictionary. Blow up the paper bag with your breath and the book will topple over.

Singing Glasses

Take a glass that is tempered (most glasses that have stems are made of tempered glass). Wet your finger and run it around the rim of the glass. The glass will begin to make a singing sound.

Take several tempered glasses and fill them to different levels with water. Then wet your finger and run it around the rim of each of the glasses. They will produce different tonal sounds. If you have several friends with you, you can even play a tune if you are a little creative.

River Crossing

Tell your friends that a section of the bridge below has been damaged. It is their job to repair the damage and make both ends meet—without drawing any lines. Ask them to try it and remind them that they cannot draw lines or fold the paper.

Let them try for a while and then show them how to do it. Have them hold the picture at arm's distance from their face. Then slowly bring the picture toward their nose while looking at the gap in the bridge. As the picture moves closer to them, the gap will close and the bridge will be repaired.

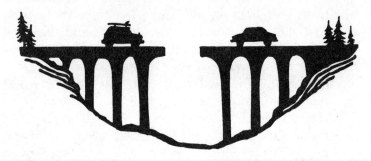

m**i**s*s* **m**at*c*h

Look carefully at the following illusion.
Which arch is larger than the other?

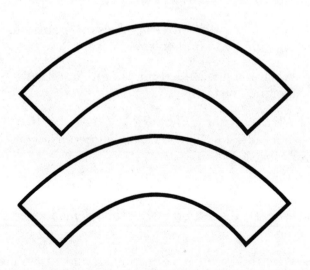

bible riddles #8

1. Why do you think the kangaroo was the most miserable animal on the Ark?

2. What prophet in the Bible was a space traveler?

3. What do you have that Cain, Abel, and Seth never had?

4. What city in the Bible has the same name of something that you find on every car?

5. When the ark landed on Mount Ararat, was Noah the first one out?

6. What was the difference between the 10,000 soldiers of Israel and the 300 soldiers Gideon chose for battle?

7. Where is the first math problem in the Bible?

8. Where is the second math problem mentioned in the Bible?

9. Why did Noah have to punish and discipline the chickens on the ark?

10. Who had the most expensive meal served in the Bible?

fun & easy magic tricks

The In-Tune Balloon

Tell your friends you have a very special balloon that is "in tune" with their thinking. This balloon will help you to come up with the right number for the group. Your friends will be wondering what you are talking about. Just say to them . . . "watch."

Take a small piece of paper and write the number 1089 on the piece of paper. Do not let your friends see what you wrote. Next, roll up the piece of paper and insert it into the "In-Tune Balloon." Now, blow up the balloon and tie a knot in the end of the balloon to hold the air and piece of paper inside. Set the balloon down in plain view in front of your friends, so they can watch it.

1. Next, have three of your friends each call out a different, single-digit number. Write those numbers down on a large piece of paper.* For example, let's

---

* The only three digit numbers this trick will not work for are numbers that are written the same backward or forward, such as: 141, 282, 363. If they select one of those numbers have them select another number. (They will think it is part of the trick.)

121

pretend that your friends called out the following numbers.

4 - 7 - 8

478

2. Reverse the numbers and subtract the smaller number from the larger.

$$\begin{array}{r} 874 \\ -478 \\ \hline 396 \end{array}$$

3. Next, reverse the answer from #2, then add the answer to #2 and the reverse of #2 together.

$$\begin{array}{r} 693 \\ + 396 \\ \hline 1089 \end{array}$$

4. Remind your friends that your balloon is so in-tune that it knows what the answer will be. Have one of your friends take a pin and pop the balloon.

5. Have him or her unroll the small piece of paper and show it to the group. They will see the number **1089** written on it. They will be amazed and impressed with your skill.

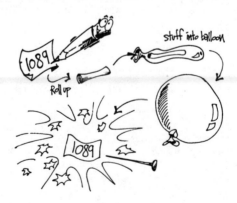

Magic Finger

You will need a small pad of paper that looks the same from both sides. On one side write three 3-digit numbers in a row. When you write the three different numbers, try and change your style of handwriting so it appears as if three different people wrote the numbers down.

259
417
632

Add the numbers together.

259
417
+ 632
―――
1308

On a different piece of paper, write down the total of the three numbers (**1308**) and seal it in an envelope. Now you are ready for the trick .

Go to a group of your friends with the pad and the envelope. Make sure that the side of the pad with the three numbers on it is facing your hand. Have three different friends write three different 3-digit numbers in a row on the blank side.

Now here is where you have to be careful. As you go to a fourth friend, turn the pad around—but don't let your friends see you turn the pad! Do it casually as you turn to the last person. Have the fourth person add up the three numbers. *These are the numbers that you originally wrote down using a different style of handwriting for each number.*

Once the last person adds the numbers together, have him tell the total to your friends. Ask them all to remember the result. Then put the pad in your pocket.

Next, pick up the envelope you've already prepared and tell your friends that you have a magic finger. You will write the answer on a piece of paper sealed inside of the envelope. Write the number 1308 on the outside of the envelope. Hand it to one of your friends to open.

They will be astounded when they open it up and find a piece of paper with the number 1308 written on it. Be sure not to let them examine your pad of paper with the numbers on both sides.

The Disappearing Glass

You will need two identically patterned handkerchiefs for this trick. You will also need some iron-on hemming tape and cardboard.

Take a glass and turn it upside down on the cardboard. With a pencil, trace around the top of the glass, drawing a circle. Cut the circle from the cardboard.

Place the cardboard in the center of one of the handkerchiefs. Form a square with the hemming tape around the cardboard circle. Don't make the square too close to the cardboard circle. Leave about a half inch on all sides. Next, put the hemming tape around the edges of the handkerchief. Carefully place the second handkerchief on top of the first one, covering the cardboard and hemming tape. Iron the two handkerchiefs together (the edges and the square around the cardboard circle).

They now look like one handkerchief (with a circle of cardboard hidden in the center). Now you are ready for the disappearing glass trick.

Sit down at a table with one of your friends at the other end. On the table will be the glass and the special handkerchief. Grab the edges of the handkerchief and show your friend that there is nothing on either side. Then place the handkerchief over the glass, making sure that the cardboard sits on the top of the rim.

Pick up the handkerchief and glass making sure that the handkerchief is still touching the top of the table. Pull the handkerchief and glass toward you while you say some magic words.

As the glass comes over your lap, let the glass drop and land in your lap. Your friend will not see it drop because the handkerchief will be touching the table and the cardboard inside will keep the glass shape. Move the handkerchief back toward your friend and all around the top of the table—still speaking your magic words. Since you are holding on to the cardboard circle, it looks like you are holding on to the glass.

HANDKERCHIEF #1

Hemming Tape

Cardboard Circle ... match Rim of Glass

Handkerchief #2

With your other hand grab the edge of the handkerchief (which is holding the cardboard circle) and jerk it out of your hand.

Show your friend both sides of the handkerchief. Your friend's mouth will drop open—he has just seen the glass disappear!

The Jumping Knot

For this trick you need two pieces of rope: one about 36" long, and the other about 6" long.

As you present this trick, fold the ends of the 6"rope together and the ends of the 36" rope together. Hold the two loops in one hand with the 6" ends going up and the 36" ends going down.

Overlap the two loops and hold them in one hand. To the audience it will appear as if you have two ropes of the same length. Tie a knot in the 6" rope. This knot will go around the loop in the 36" rope. Pull the knot tight. To

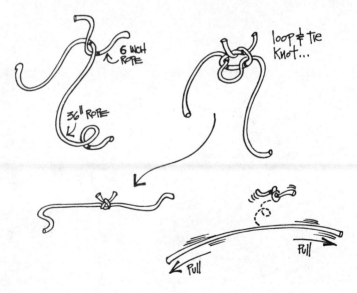

the audience it will look as if you have tied the two equal-length ropes in a knot.

Next, grab the ends of the 36" rope and let the audience see the knot. Tell your friends that this is a magic jumping knot. Say some magic words, and yank on both ends of the 36" rope. The knot will "jump" off. Your friends will be surprised!

Toothpick Magic

This trick will be lots of fun and it will really fool your friends.

You will need a handkerchief with a hem and a wooden toothpick for this trick.

You will need to prepare ahead of time by slipping a toothpick into the hem of the clean handkerchief. Make sure it fits loosely enough that you can move it around. Now you are ready to have a good time.

When you are with your friend, pull out a wooden toothpick and set it on the table in front of you. Next, pull out your special handkerchief. Show your friend that there is nothing on either side. Be sure that you are holding on to the toothpick in the hem as you flip the handkerchief around.

Have your friend place the toothpick on the table in the center of the handkerchief. Next, fold the edges of the handkerchief over the toothpick. Pick up the handkerchief and pretend to search for the toothpick your friend dropped in. In reality, you are moving the toothpick in the hem to the top of the handkerchief while moving the toothpick your friend dropped into a lower position.

Once you have moved the toothpick in

Toothpick
in Hem

the hem to the top, let your friend feel the toothpick in the cloth. (Your friend will be feeling the toothpick in the hem.) Then have him break the toothpick several times. Say some magic words over the handkerchief as you place it on the table.

Tell your friend that your special magic will restore the broken toothpick to its original length—and make it whole again.

Grab the edges of the handkerchief and shake out the toothpick your friend dropped in. He will be flabbergasted! He will ask you how you did it! Be sure not to let him feel the broken toothpick still in the hem of the handkerchief.

The Great Production Box

This is a trick that will bring the house down. It will blow away your friends and family. It is one of the best production tricks an amateur can perform.

You will need two large cardboard boxes for this trick. The boxes must be large enough to comfortably hold an adult in them when open. They should be about 30 to 36 inches high. The boxes must be wider than a doorway. You will need an assistant and some items to pull out of the box. You also need to have two folding chairs you can stand on.

One of the cardboard boxes should be a *little* smaller than the other one. Make sure the larger box will slip over the smaller box. Cut a square hole in the back side of the smaller box. It has to be large enough for an adult person to crawl through. You can paint the boxes if you like. Unpainted boxes, however, will really catch the audience off-guard. They will think that they are plain, folded boxes.

You will need a special room that is prepared before your audience enters. Your assistant will be hidden from view: She can be hiding behind something in the room or be in another room entirely.

Now for the presentation of the trick:

Get your audience seated and tell them you have something special to show them. Once your audience is ready, briefly step out of the room and grab your two boxes. Have them folded flat with the smaller box in front and the larger box in back. The hole in the smaller box should be against the larger box, hidden from the audience.

Walk into the room or onto the stage with the folded boxes under your arm. As you come in, turn around as you are talking. This will let your audience see that you are only carrying folded boxes and nothing could be in them.

Set the folded boxes in front of an open doorway, leaning against the doorway. Talk to the audience about your special boxes: Where you found them—at the supermarket or some other place.

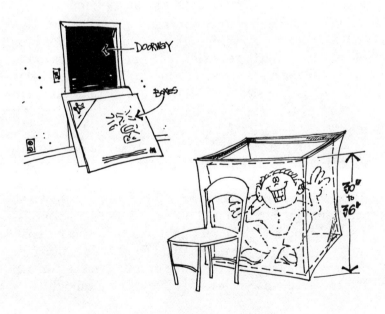

Slide out the larger box, leaving the smaller one leaning against the doorway. Walk across the room with the larger box and open it up so that it forms a square. Go back to the smaller box and open it up so that it forms a square. The smaller box is now facing the hallway or opening to another room where your assistant is hiding.

As you walk back to the larger box keep talking and making up a story about the box. Make it wild and funny and keep their attention on the larger box by moving it while you are talking.

In the meantime, your assistant will be crawling into the smaller box. She should bring some items to pull out of the box with her. As she crawls through the opening she will have to be careful not to move the box or rise up too high to be seen from the top.

After you have given your assistant enough time to crawl into the smaller box, pick up the larger box and carry it over to the smaller box. It is all right to let your audience see through the open top and bottom.

Place (slide) the larger box over the smaller box. This move will now cover the opening on the smaller box. Slowly drag both boxes to the center of the stage or room, talking all the while to distract the audience from what is happening. The slowness allows your assistant to move forward within the box without the box hitting her body and giving away the trick.

Once in the center of the room, turn the box around (in one spot) so that the audience sees all sides. Then ask them what they would like to see you pull out of the box. They will say all kinds of weird things. Ignore them and reach into the box and pull out one of the items your assistant brought with her. It might be a Teddy bear, a coat, an old shoe, toys, or whatever you would like to pull out. After you have pulled out three or four items, again ask the audience what they would like you to pull out.

This time, tell them you have something special. Grab a chair that you have placed in the room and put it in front of the box. This will get their curiosity up. Then grab the second chair you have placed in the room. Place it inside the box (Don't hit your assistant!) Your audience will be wondering what is going on. Take one last look at the audience and make whatever comment you would like—then reach over into the box, grab the hand of your assistant, and have her stand on the chair in the box. your audience will go wild. Have your assistant step on the chair outside the box and down to the ground. (Why the chairs? Remember, the box is 30 to 36 inches high, which is very hard to step over. It wouldn't be good if your assistant accidentally knocked over the box and let the audience see the hole in the smaller box.)

As soon as your assistant is out of the box. Bow and thank the audience. Quickly fold the two boxes together and walk out of the room with them. You don't want your audience to discover your secret.

Have loads of fun with this one.

The Great Coin Vanish

This trick will work with any size of coin you can hide in your hand. The trick is to rub a coin into your forearm until it vanishes.

You can start the trick by telling your friend that you have a very special magic coin that you are going to rub into your arm. Put your left elbow on the table with your left hand on your neck. The trick is even more effective if you have a short-sleeved shirt on.

With your right hand, pick up the coin and begin rubbing your left forearm. Tell your friend that if you rub hard enough the coin will vanish into your arm.

In the process of rubbing, accidentally drop the coin on the table. Don't make a big deal of it, just pick it up with your left hand. Pretend to put it into your right hand and begin rubbing again. While your friend is watching your right hand rub the coin into your arm, you will really have the coin in your left hand. Place your left hand up by your neck as before—except this time you will drop the coin into your shirt collar.

Once the coin is safely in your shirt collar, move your hand away from your neck and look down at your forearm. You can say to your friend, "I think it is almost gone."

As you make the final rub on your left forearm move your right hand away and blow at your arm like you blew the coin away. This is to distract your friend even more. Open both of your hands and show him that the coin has vanished.

While he is looking around for the coin, you can put your left hand back up by your neck. If the coin has not slipped down your shirt you can grab it with the fingers of your left hand. Bring your hand forward and make a motion by your friend's left ear. Say, "Here it is," and pretend to pull the coin from his ear. He will be fooled twice.

Pounding the Quarter

You can do this classic trick of misdirection at a restaurant or at almost any dinner table. All you need is a quarter, a salt shaker, and some paper napkins.

Tell your friend that you're going to put a quarter on the table and then pound the quarter through the table with the salt shaker.

Make sure your friend is sitting at the opposite end of the table from you. Put the quarter on the table in front of you. Place the salt shaker on top of the quarter. Open up the paper napkins and place them over the salt shaker. Put enough napkins over the salt shaker so that you cannot see the salt shaker. You can tell your friend that putting the napkins on the salt shaker helps to keep your hand from becoming hurt in case the salt shaker breaks. Squeeze the napkins tight around the salt shaker.

After you have squeezed the napkins tight, tap the quarter a few times with the salt shaker like you are getting ready to really hit it. Each time you tap the quarter draw the salt shaker back toward you—just barely above table top. Draw it back once and look at the quarter. Move the salt shaker back toward the quarter and tap it a couple of more times. The second time you draw the covered salt shaker back toward your chest, quietly and carefully let the salt shaker slip out of the napkins and drop into your lap. Make sure you hold the napkins like the salt shaker is still inside! Bring the empty napkins back over the quarter and gently set them down. They should keep the same shape because you wrapped them tightly at the beginning.

Say to your friend, "Here we go." Don't hesitate—pound the paper napkins down hard and flat. It will make a loud noise. Your friend is expecting the quarter to go through the table and not the salt shaker.

At the same time you are pounding the napkins with one hand, grab the salt shaker with the other hand. Hold the salt shaker under the table at about the same location where the quarter is on the table. As soon as the napkins are flat, begin to pull the salt shaker out from under the table. It will make it look like you pounded the salt shaker through the table and caught it with your other hand. Say, "Oops—I pushed the wrong thing through!" Your friend will be in shock. He won't believe you actually pushed anything through the table!

Mental Magic

This is a trick that can be performed almost anywhere as long as you have the following numbers with you. Write these numbers on a card in the same order as they are given, so your card looks *exactly* like this.

1	2	4	8
7	6	13	10
5	3	15	14
3	15	7	13
11	7	6	15
9	10	5	12
13	14	12	11
15	11	14	9

Hand the card to your friends and have them look at the numbers. Tell them to select a number as a group and not tell you what the number is. All you want them to do is tell you which column(s) their number is in. If their number is in more than one column, they should tell you which columns it's in: column #1, #2, #3, or #4.

As soon as they let you know which column (or columns) their selected number is in, you can tell them what it is. All you have to do is add together the top numbers on the card of the column(s) their number is in—that will be their selection.

For example, let's say that your friends selected the number 6. The number 6 is in columns #2 and #3. The top two numbers are 2 and 4. Added together they are six. It is that simple for you. It will be very confusing to your friends. They will wonder how you did this great mental magic.

The Multicolored Balloon

To prepare for this trick, you need two balloons of different colors. Carefully stuff the light-colored balloon inside the dark-colored balloon. Leave enough of the light-colored balloon sticking out so you can blow it up.

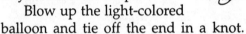

Blow up the light-colored balloon and tie off the end in a knot. Take a pencil with an eraser and gently shove the knot of the light-colored balloon inside of the dark-colored balloon with the eraser.

Now blow up the dark-colored balloon so that it is a little bigger than the light-colored balloon.

Tell you friends that you have a magic multicolored balloon. Then take a pin and pop the dark-colored balloon. The balloon will seem to change colors before their eyes.

Be careful that you don't poke too hard and pop both balloons at the same time.

The World's Greatest Card Trick

· This may very well be the world's greatest amateur card trick!

Take a deck of cards and allow anyone to shuffle the deck. After he or she is finished, take the deck and fan the cards. Allow a friend to select any card. Tell him you will turn your back while he shows it to his other friends.

As the card is being shown to the other friends, split the deck, with half of the cards being in each hand. Memorize the card on the bottom of the deck in your left hand. When you turn around, have your friend place his card on top of the cards in your right hand. Now place the cards in your left hand on top of his card. *You now have your memorized card directly on top of the selected card.*

With all of the cards in one hand, cut a few of the cards off the bottom of the deck and move them to the top of the deck. Then cut a few of the cards off the top of the deck and put them on the bottom of the deck. This is done to misdirect your friends. *In reality, you have not changed the position of your memorized card in the middle of the deck. It is still on top of the selected card.*

Now turn the deck face up, so you can see the different cards. Begin to look through the cards (you can fan them out) until you see your memorized card. Now memorize the card directly in front of it. It is your friend's selected card. Don't forget what it is.

Next, hand the cards to anyone in the group and have him or her shuffle the deck. It doesn't matter how much he or she shuffles the deck; you still know which card your friend selected.

Take the deck back. Look at the faces of the cards and begin to move the cards into different positions in the deck. This is done to help you move your friend's selected card to the top of the deck. After moving five or six cards around, move your friend's card to the top. No one in the group will know what you are doing. Then move a few more cards into the middle and stop.

There are two secrets to this fantastic trick. The first is to move your friend's card to the top of the deck. The second is as follows. Take a piece of scotch tape and reverse it so that it sticks to itself. Make the reverse loop big enough to go around your thumb. Take the scotch tape with the sticky side out and remove it from your thumb and place it between the first and second knuckle on the ring finger of your left hand.

No one will see the tape loop on your left hand while you are doing the trick. Your fingers will be slightly bent when you hold cards in your left hand. Everyone will be watching you move cards and trying to remember the selected card.

After you finally move your friend's selected card to the top of the deck, hold the deck in your left hand. Keep your ring finger slightly bent so that the sticky loop of tape does not stick to any of the cards.

Now, here is when the fun really begins. With your right hand begin to go through the cards. Go about a third of the way into the deck. Hold this group of cards in your right hand and show the group the card that is on the bottom of the deck in your left hand. Say, "Here is your selected card." The entire group will say that it is not the card. Look very perplexed, and ask, "Are you sure?" They will tell you they are sure that it is the wrong card.

Then continue to go through a few more cards in your left hand, passing them to the right hand. Stop and show them another card. With a big smile say, "I found it. Here is your card." They will say that it is not the selected card. Then you say, "It has to be." They will all say it is not.

Now, with more determination go through a few more cards and stop. Pass the cards from your left hand to your right. With an impressive motion show your friends the card in your left hand. Say, "This has to be it."

They will all laugh and make different comments and say that it is not the selected card.

After the third time of showing the wrong card, straighten out your ring finger with the reverse sticky tape on it. Flatten the tape on the back of the top card. It is your friend's selected card.

Look very upset. Pretend to be mad. Slam the cards in your right hand back together with the cards in your left hand. Once they are joined back together, take the entire deck with your right hand and slide the sticky tape off your ring finger.

The sticky tape is now on your friend's selected card on the top of the deck. No one will be looking at the deck. They will be watching you because you are upset.

Now for the final move that will bring the house down! Take the deck of cards and turn toward a wall in the room that is flat and does not have any pictures on it. Take the deck and say, "I hate these dumb card tricks." Try and make it sound as if you are serious. Throw the entire deck at the flat wall. Make sure the card on top hits the wall first. Be sure that you do not have to throw the cards more than about three feet. What will happen?

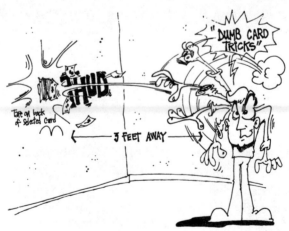

The deck of cards will slam into the wall. The force of your throw and the weight of the deck will make the sticky tape flatten out and stick the selected card to the wall. All of the rest of the cards will fall to the floor.

As you throw the deck and it hits the wall, quickly turn and walk away from the wall, pretending to be in a mad huff. Go across the room and sit down in a chair, still pretending to be upset.

It will take a second or two before someone will see your friend's selected card sticking on the wall. He will yell, and everyone will turn to look. They will be absolutely astounded when they see the selected card on the wall. And all the time they thought that you blew the trick, you were sucking them further into your fantastic magic ability. This trick will be talked about for weeks afterward. Be sure to never tell your friends how you did it.

answer key

Brain-Benders (page 11)

1. None. In total darkness it is impossible to see anything.
2. The woman was the judge who performed the marriage ceremonies.
3. None of them. You can't find unlisted phone numbers in a phone book.
4. Australia.
5. If Danny had truly discovered a liquid that would instantly dissolve anything it touches, it would have dissolved the flask he was holding.
6. A wedding ring.
7. A coffin.
8. The great golfer was bald.
9. None—Moses never was on the ark—Noah was.
10. Before Willard discovered the fly, he had put sugar in his coffee and taken a sip. When the new cup of coffee arrived at his table he took a sip and tasted the sugar in it.
11. Mr. Know-it-All said, "The answer is simple. There is only one groove, otherwise the record would end after the first song. The same groove leads the needle to the next song . . . and so forth . . . until all of the songs have been played."
12. The hunter was starting to cross a bridge when he saw the tiger. He ran toward the tiger to get off the bridge before running to the river that was below the bridge.
13. The letter E.

14. The bookworm travels 16 inches. When a book stands on a shelf in front of you, its front cover is on the right side and its back cover is on the left. The worm travels, therefore, along the 16-inch path shown by the dotted line below.

Vol 1	Vol 2	Vol 3	Vol 4	Vol 5	Vol 6	Vol 7	Vol 8	Vol 9	Vol 10

15. All of them. In the case of 7, it can be divided into two parts, each being $3\frac{1}{2}$.

16. Mr. West showed little concern because it was only a coin in his pocket.

17. 1. U: Fit as a fiddle.
    2. J: Flat as a pancake.
    3. P: Blind as a bat.
    4. S: Light as a feather.
    5. L: Happy as a hog in new mud.
    6. V: Cold as ice.
    7. R: Cool as a cucumber.
    8. Z: Fat as a hog.
    9. E: Poor as a church mouse.
    10. O: Rich as a king.
    11. Q: Patient as Job.
    12. T: Stubborn as a mule.
    13. C: Proud as a peacock.
    14. W: Dead as a doornail.
    15. D: Hard as a rock.
    16. H: Soft as silk.
    17. B: Clear as a bell.
    18. F: Slippery as an eel.
    19. A: Sharp as a razor.
    20. I: Smart as a whip.
    21. X: Clean as a whistle.
    22. K: Pleased as punch.
    23. Y: Busy as a bee.
    24. G: Neat as a pin.
    25. M: Sound as a dollar.
    26. N: Thick as thieves.

Bible Riddles #1 (page 16)

1. Is Me. Isaiah said, "Woe is me."
2. Adam.
3. In Acts 1:14—"These all continued with one accord."
4. Some people believe that it was Zacchaeus. Others believe it was Nehemiah (Ne-high-a-miah), or Bildad the Shuhite (Shoe-height). But in reality it was Peter the disciple. He slept on his watch (Matthew 26:40).
5. In John 3:7—Jesus said to Nicodemus, "Marvel not" (Marblenot).
6. Their paradise (pair-o-dice) was taken away from them.
7. In Matthew 28:20—"Lo (Low), I am with you always" (not high up in the air).
8. "Now I herd everything."
9. When he slept with his forefathers (Genesis 49:29).

Word Quiz #1 (page 22)

1. Mystery.
2. Scrambled eggs.
3. Hands up.
4. Dig for clues.
5. Double agent.
6. You are under arrest.
7. Corner the crook.
8. Wake up in the middle of the night.
9. Partners in crime.

Crazy Picture Quiz #1 (page 23)

1. A spider hitching a ride on a rocket to the moon.
2. A pig sticking his nose through a hole in the fence.
3. A clumsy elephant walking a tightrope in the circus.
4. Pin the tail on the donkey.

Bible Riddles #2 (page 31)

1. Eve's appearance for Adam's benefit.
2. In Proverbs 13:24—"He that spareth his rod hateth his son."
3. Because many men get in by a close shave.
4. Noah—he floated his stock while the whole world was in liquidation.

5. Fallen arches.
6. They raised Cain.
7. The widow's "mite" (Mark 12:42 NKJV) and the "wicked flee" (Proverbs 28:1).
8. On Noah's Ark.
9. Blinds.
10. When the evil spirits entered the swine (Matthew 8:30-32).

Word Quiz #2 (page 39)

1. Neon lights.
2. Prosperity around the corner.
3. Paradox.
4. Yield right of way.
5. 2 peas in a pod.
6. The price is right.
7. Horsing around.
8. Pizza with everything on it.
9. 20 below zero.

Crazy Picture Quiz #2 (page 40)

1. A man with an umbrella riding a bike.
2. A hopscotch highway.
3. A skateboarding elephant.
4. A box of straws viewed from the top with only one straw left.

Bible Riddles #3 (page 47)

1. Eve—when she gave Adam a little Cain.
2. Where the Lord gives Moses two tablets.
3. In 2 Kings 21:13: "And I will wipe Jerusalem as a man wipeth a dish, wiping it, and turning it upside down."
4. On the head.
5. Because he broke the ten commandments all at once.
6. Job—he cursed the day he was born.
7. A little before Eve.
8. Joshua, the son of Nun.
9. When Joseph served in Pharaoh's court.
10. Yes, the duck took a bill, the frog took a greenback, and the skunk took a scent.

Bible Riddles #4 (page 52)

1. He was a baker. We know this because he went to Philippi (fill-a-pie).
2. Because it had no Eve.
3. Because she was dissatisfied with her Lot (see Genesis 19).
4. The story about the fellow who loafs and fishes.
5. She had sufficient grounds to stay away.
6. Job—he had the most patience.
7. Because the Lord said to multiply on the face of the earth.
8. As long as he was Abel.
9. Noah—when he took his family and the animals out of the ark. It made the ark (arc) light.
10. Cain—when he hit Abel.

Pick These (page 53)

Through the Goalposts (page 53)

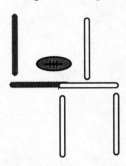

Double Sixes (page 53)

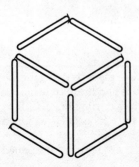

The Exploding Star (page 54)

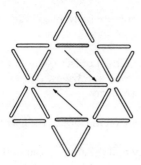

Nine to five (page 54)

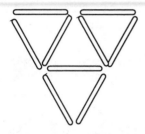

What's Your Angle (page 55)
   Triangle

Thought Twisters (page 56)

1. They were not playing against each other.
2. Are becomes area.
3. Because it makes the ear hear.
4. An angle.
5. None—the others will fly away.
6. Short.
7. One.
8. The clever thief was able to steal all three ropes by doing the following things. First, he tied the left rope and the middle rope in
   a knot at the bottom before he started climbing. He then
   climbed up the left rope till he got to the left hook. He wrapped
   his legs around the left rope so that he would not slip. He then
   reached over and untied the center rope. He pushed the untied

end of the center rope through the hook until the knot at the bottom of the left and middle ropes arrived at the middle hook. He then grabbed both ropes hanging on the middle hook and moved over and held on to both of them. He reached back and untied the left rope. That end fell to the ground. He then reached over and untied the right rope and it fell to the ground. He then slid down the double ropes hanging from the middle hook. When he reached the ground he pulled on one of the ropes and pulled down both the left rope and the middle rope. He then quietly left King Midas' palace.

9.

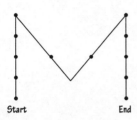

10. The word is *news*. The arrows represent North, East, West, and South.
11. An ear of corn.
12. Neither one—the yolk of the eggs is yellow.
13. Eleven minutes—only eleven cuts are needed.
14. The man in the black hat. Truth-teller or not, the man in the white hat would answer yes. Why? If he were a truth-teller, obviously he would tell the truth and say yes. If he were a liar, he would lie and say yes. Therefore, since the man in the black hat said that the man in the white hat would say yes, the man in the black hat must be the truth-teller and the man in the white hat the liar.
15. The same reason you cannot take the picture of a man with a wooden leg anywhere in the world. You need a camera—not a wooden leg—to take pictures.
16. Halfway—then the black bear would be running out of the woods.
17. 1. F. Tighten
    2. G. Plenty
    3. H. Ascent
    4. O. Partial

5. K. Unknown
6. D. Select
7. A. Inadequate
8. E. Power
9. B. Reward
10. N. Join
11. M. Appear
12. J. Colorful
13. L. Plain
14. C. Clumsiness
15. I. Idle

Word Quiz #3 (page 60)

1. Banana split.
2. Swear on a stack of Bibles.
3. Hole in one.
4. Turn of the century.
5. Backgammon.
6. Bet one's bottom dollar.
7. Forty-niner.
8. Unfinished business.
9. GI overseas.

Crazy Picture Quiz #3 (page 71)

1. Hang-gliding snail.
2. An unhappy man who fell into a vat of motor oil.
3. Coat hangers for those who have nothing to wear.
4. Two ships trying to rescue a drowning reindeer.

Bible Riddles #5 (page 72)

1. Down in the mouth.
2. They both come before the fall.
3. You can't keep a good man down.
4. Because David rocked Goliath to sleep.
5. One was a high ark and the other is a hierarch.
6. When she pulled his ears (Ruth 2:2).
7. On the side of his head.
8. Adam—he was first in the human race.
9. Because he would be several thousand years old.
10. He had Ham (Genesis 7:13).

Bible Riddles #6 (page 84)

1. To avoid Egyptian traffic.
2. Samson—he brought the house down.
3. Jonah—even the great fish couldn't keep him down.
4. First and second Samuel.
5. Genesis 1:1—in the beginning (big inning).
   Genesis 3:6—Eve stole first and Adam stole second.
   Luke 15:11-32—the prodigal son made a home run.
   Ezekiel 36:12—"Yea, I will cause men to walk."
6. Eve.
7. Because he had such miserable comforters (Job 16:2).
8. At the bank of the Red Sea.
9. Because Mrs. Noah sat on the deck.

Word Quiz #4 (page 90)

1. Growing pains.
2. Man overboard.
3. 4-wheel drive.
4. Downtown.
5. Double or nothing.
6. 3 degrees below zero.
7. Sitting duck.
8. High chair.
9. Bridge over troubled waters.

Brain-Benders (page 91)

1. A glass house after a stone was thrown at it.
2. A lonely hotdog looking for the mustard.
3. A giraffe that swallowed a phone.
4. Two boys blowing up balloons out of their apartment windows.

Bible Riddles #7 (page 96)

1. Joseph—Pharaoh made a ruler out of him.
2. The chicken, of course. God doesn't lay eggs.
3. When Pharaoh's daughter took a little prophet (profit) from the bulrushes.
4. The wages of sin.

5. Early in the fall.
6. His father was Enoch. Enoch never died he was translated to heaven (Hebrews 11:5).
7. Isaiah 40:25—God has never seen His equal, Abraham Lincoln seldom saw his equal, and we see our equals every day.
8. Quackers.
9. Because he went to the land of Nod (Genesis 4:16).
10. At the banks of the Jordan.

Four Coins in a Row (page 103)

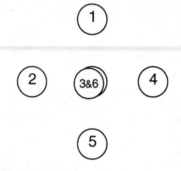

Word Quiz #5 (page 104)

1. Split level.
2. Little league.
3. I understand.
4. Paradise.
5. Touchdown.
6. Total loss.
7. Writers cramp.
8. Six feet under ground.
9. Check-out counter.

Crazy Picture Quiz #5 (page 105)

1. Fat man diving off diving board with an umbrella.
2. Two nuns enjoying a fountain.
3. A quarter and a dime standing on edge on a table.
4. A man who stood too close to the elevator door.

Mind Warpers (page 106)

1. Rollerskates.
2. None of them—horses can't talk.
3. The snakes ate each other up; we have no idea where they went.
4. The old farmer took the rabbit across and left the fox with the lettuce. He then went back and picked up the lettuce. That left the fox alone. Upon arriving on the side with the rabbit, he left the lettuce and took the rabbit back with him. When he got to the side with the fox, he dropped off the rabbit and took the fox across, leaving it with the lettuce. He then crossed back to his original starting point and brought the rabbit back with him to the other side.
5. The letter "p" is the middle in "the alphabet."
6. Horse racing.
7. It would take the beetle 28 days to crawl out of the well. On the twenty-eighth day the beetle reaches the top of the well. Once there, it does not, of course, slip backward.
8. None—the pirate ship would rise with the tide.
9. Old Pete added his horse to the group making it 18 horses. The oldest son took half, which is 9 horses. The second son took 6 horses, which is one-third. The youngest son took 2 horses, which is one-ninth. When you add, 9, 6, and 2, you get 17 horses. Old Pete then jumped on his horse and rode off.
10. Usher: us/ she/ he/ her.
11. Hijinks.
12. An hour-and-a-quarter equals 75 minutes.
13. The young man was an accomplished juggler. When he came to the beam he began to juggle the one pound lead weights. By doing this he always kept one of the lead weights in the air.
14. You will find that the words "mistakes" and "fooled" were misspelled. The third mistake was that a third mistake wasn't put in the sentences.
15. None—it's Alexander Hamilton who was never president.
16. I'm underpaid and overworked.
17. Underground.

The Puzzling Pyramids (page 111)

There are 18 puzzling pyramids.

Bible Riddles #8 (page 120)

1. Because her children had to play inside during the rain.
2. Elijah—he went up in a fiery chariot (2 Kings 2:11).
3. Grandparents.
4. Tyre (tire).
5. No—he came forth (fourth) out of the ark.
6. 9,700.
7. Genesis 1:4—when God divided the light from the darkness.
8. Genesis 1:28—when God told Adam and Eve to go forth and multiply.
9. Because they were using fowl (foul) language.
10. Esau—it cost him his birthright (Genesis 25:33).

Other Books by Bob Phillips

World's Greatest Collection of
Clean Jokes

The Return of the Good
Clean Jokes

The World's Greatest Collection
of Heavenly Humor

The World's Greatest Collection of
Riddles and Daffy Definitions

The World's Greatest Collection of
Knock, Knock Jokes and
Tongue Twisters

The Best of the Good Clean Jokes

Wit and Wisdom

Humor Is Tremendous

The All-New Clean Joke Book

Good Clean Jokes for Kids

The Encyclopedia of
Good Clean Jokes

Ultimate Good Clean
Jokes for Kids

Awesome Good Clean
Jokes for Kids

More Awesome Good Clean
Jokes for Kids

Wacky Good Clean Jokes for Kids

Nutty Good Clean Jokes for Kids

Loony Good Clean Jokes for Kids

Crazy Good Clean Jokes for Kids

Goofy Good Clean Jokes for Kids
Bible Brainteasers

The Great Bible Challenge

The Awesome Book of
Bible Trivia

How Can I Be Sure?

Anger Is a Choice

Redi-Reference

Redi-Reference Daily
Bible-Reading Plan

The Delicate Art of Dancing
with Porcupines

God's Hand over Hume

Praise Is a Three-Lettered
Word—Joy

Friendship, Love & Laughter

Phillips' Book of Great Quotes
& Funny Sayings

The All-American Quote Book

Bible Olympics

Big Book—The Bible—Questions
and Answers

The Unofficial Liberal Joke Book

What to Do Until the
Psychiatrist Comes

For information on how to purchase any of the above books, contact
your local bookstore or send a self-addressed stamped envelope to:
Family Services
P.O. Box 9363
Fresno, CA 93702

Dear Reader,

We would appreciate hearing from you regarding this Harvest House nonfiction book. It will enable us to continue to give you the best in Christian publishing.

1. What most influenced you to purchase *Tricks, Stunts, and Good Clean Fun?*
   - ❑ Author
   - ❑ Subject matter
   - ❑ Backcover copy
   - ❑ Recommendations
   - ❑ Cover/Title
   - ❑ Other_____

2. Where did you purchase this book?
   - ❑ Christian bookstore
   - ❑ General bookstore
   - ❑ Department store
   - ❑ Grocery store
   - ❑ Other_____

3. Your overall rating of this book?
   ❑ Excellent ❑ Very good ❑ Good ❑ Fair ❑ Poor

4. How likely would you be to purchase other books by this author?
   ❑ Very likely ❑ Not very likely ❑ Somewhat likely ❑ Not at all

5. What types of books most interest you? (Check all that apply.)
   - ❑ Women's Books
   - ❑ Marriage Books
   - ❑ Current Issues
   - ❑ Christian Living
   - ❑ Bible Studies
   - ❑ Fiction
   - ❑ Biographies
   - ❑ Children's Books
   - ❑ Youth Books
   - ❑ Other_____

6. Please check the box next to your age group.
   ❑ Under 18 ❑ 18-24 ❑ 25-34 ❑ 35-44 ❑ 45-54 ❑ 55 and over

Mail to: Editorial Director
Harvest House Publishers
1075 Arrowsmith
Eugene, OR 97402

Name _____

Address _____

State _____ Zip _____

Thank you for helping us to help you in future publications!